MY LIFE

OF MIRACLES

31 True Stories to help you anchor
your hope and trust in God

Brittany Turpin

First Edition July 2018

Library of Congress Cataloging-in-Publication Data: 2018907364 Control Number for My Life Of Miracles ISBN: 9781720996675

Editor Ellis Weiner
Cover design by Lauren Caughlan
Author Photograph by Tyler Klee
Author makeup by Sabina Turpin

Speaking engagement inquiries email author at brittanyturpin@aol.com

Dedication

I am not really sure if this is the only book I'll write or the first of many, so I want to make sure that I cover everyone, or most everyone, that I am thankful for--obviously starting off with God. I am very thankful that You are my guiding light and that, so many times, You have made an occasionally very sad life joyful. For that I will always serve You! Next, to my husband, Steven, for loving me when I was broken and being the glue that helped heal me. I'm also thankful for my amazing children, Lauren, Sabina, Blake, and Chandler, for adding to my life laughter and love such as I never knew before. My Aunt Betty: No words of gratitude could ever express how thankful I am for your showing me how wonderful life could be, just by being you! My wonderful mother-in-law, Sabina: You have been a girlfriend and mother, and mostly an answered prayer. Thank you for always being a blessing in our lives. Tom Sullivan, my father-in-law: The rock of the family. Thank you for your overwhelming love and generosity, it never ceases to amaze me. My father, for showing me the value of forgiveness. And, last but not least, to my many friends, who have enhanced my life with love.

Table of Contents

Introduction

I am not a professional writer. I have never once thought, "I can't wait to write a book!" It was the opposite, actually--I fought for many years the impulse to write this. But I knew, as sure as I breathed, that this was what I was supposed to do!

The chapters are not in chronological order. Honestly, I wrote them in an order, and in a way, so I could weather the after-effects of writing each one. Some were very hard to write, and took me months before I could heal from having written them. Sometimes I could only write about the funny stuff. I thought about putting them in the right historical order, but then I felt that the result wouldn't be legitimate in terms of feeling.

In any case, I hope I wrote this well enough for you to take away one thing: Make God your best friend. Listen to Him. I pray a lot. Very little of it is on my knees or crying with my eyes closed. I talk to God wherever I am. I talk to Him about everything. But I also listen. I hope this book teaches you to do exactly that!

In closing, I would especially like to thank Him for His willingness to allow me to suffer--because in the end, God's plan always worked out for the good!

Foreword

Brittany Turpin is a wonderful friend. I'm talking about that friend who calls you when you think about them; the friend who shows up at your door with a meal before you even realize you needed it. She is the person you call if you want the pure, unadulterated truth. After reading her book, I know why. Actually, I always thought I knew why, but reading the story of miraculous intervention in her life just solidified it. Brittany Turpin walks with God. She hears God's voice and she actually acts on what she hears.

We live in a day and age where we are constantly barraged with voices. We hear them through our smartphones, satellite radio, cable TV, and the internet. These voices are often delivering the disappointing news of the day or even a story with disturbing elements. Oftentimes even the current music we hear is uncomfortable and makes us long for the uplifting music of our youth. With the 24- hour news cycle and the internet, not only do we get to hear bad news over and over, but we can get in depth information on it by doing a simple search in a search engine—some of it true, some of it "fake news". All of this can lead to a feeling of hopelessness or even despair. In the midst of this I, probably like many of you, find myself gravitating toward people who are positive and uplifting. That's how I got to know Brittany.

When we first met as swim moms, I could tell that this was a woman who had lived through some things and was the better for her life experiences. The way she parents— loving, encouraging, and empowering—is an almost tangible force, and it speaks volumes about who she is. She loves her husband and extended family with that same force. In my mind she had either grown up with that kind of influence in her life, or learned it through some experiences. I was blessed to find out more of who she is when I went through my own life crisis. I know she heard God speaking, because she would call with a word of encouragement or show up at my door at just the right time—every time. It was almost uncanny.

When you read this book, the story of how one woman learned to listen to that quiet inner voice and be blessed by it, you are getting a taste of the real woman. Brittany doesn't hold anything back. She hears the most loving and encouraging voice of all, and although she doesn't always like what he speaks to her, she is faithful to act on it and it hasn't failed her yet.

Brittany's collection of stories is not a book of exceptions and it isn't meant to be. It is a book full of real life examples of how we normal, everyday people can listen, hear, and follow the voice of God and be blessed by it. I hope you take in the stories and are as encouraged as I have been to tune in to the only voice truly worth listening to; the one that empowers us to love, forgive, choose joy, and respond in ways that leave a lasting impact on us and our little corner of the world.

Yolanda Weinberger

Radio Personality

Chapter 1

Appendix

(Most books put a section called "Appendix" at the back, after all the main material. This one will put "Appendix" at the start. You'll see why.)

I really don't remember what age I was--maybe eight. But that's the only part of this story that I don't remember fully and have down cold.

I woke up in the middle of the night and I could barely breathe. Every time I took a breath I would just shriek in pain. This was a bad thing because, as you know, breathing is *very important*. You want to be able to do it as painlessly as possible for pretty much your entire life.

I was shaking, shuddering, and vibrating to the point where my teeth were chattering. The fever was so high, beads of sweat just rolled off me.

How bad was it? *I couldn't even cry.* I was in way too much pain—and when I say "pain," bear in mind that I have had four children and zero C-sections. My average labor time was 20 hours plus. That's almost a full day (each) of childbirth—which, as you may have heard, is usually a very painful experience and is no one's idea of "fun."

But they were nothing like this. In fact, just telling this story now, decades later, makes me cringe. The memory of how small and helpless I was when this nightmare began, and of what happened—or didn't happen—next, is still bewildering.

My side hurt. I rolled out of bed and crawled like a wounded dog toward the stairs. It took forever, or maybe it just felt that way. In any case, I got there with the idea of calling out to my father.

I called and called, but got no answer. So I set forth on the impossible, epic journey of going downstairs. I don't know how long it took--crawling down those stairs, trying to make progress but also to keep myself from pitching forward and tumbling to the bottom and, worst of all, having to *keep breathing*--but it felt like a lifetime. I was miserable and desolate and wanted to throw up. I was literally afraid I was going to die.

I finally reached the bottom and realized that I could smell alcohol--he had been drinking. I made my way to my father's bed. Desperately, I pulled the covers off and moaned, "Dad, please wake up." I asked and begged and pleaded to be taken to the hospital.

"What's wrong with you?" he said.

I told him I couldn't breathe, and that my side was in horrible pain. Again, I pleaded to go to the hospital.

"Go back to bed," he said. "You'll feel better in the morning."

I must have begged him for ten minutes. But I knew he was never going to take me. He was old school: Just go to sleep and everything will be ok in the morning! Remember, I was eight. What little kid ever willingly asks to go to the hospital? I never did. But at that moment, even I knew something terrible was going on inside me, and I needed serious help.

Finally, I gave up. As though having to hike up a mountain on my hands and knees, I crawled back up the stairs. Usually a return trip feels much shorter than an outbound trip. But not this time. This, too, felt like it took hours.

Finally, I made it and crawled back into bed. As I lay there, I knew that, if I didn't do something immediately, I was going to die. I just knew it in my heart. So I sat up and did the only thing that was available to me. I prayed.

It sure wasn't my first prayer. But I can say that, from that moment to the present, it was one of the most real, sincere prayers that I have ever prayed in my life.

With all my heart, I asked God to please not let me die. I told Him that I wanted to grow up, and get married someday, and to be a mommy. I asked Him, over and over, to please, please not let me die.

The next thing I knew it was morning.

I woke up and realized that I felt perfectly fine. I got up. I got dressed. I had breakfast. I played with my brother and sister as though none of the previous night's torment had ever happened.

Fast forward six years, to the ninth grade. I was in Biology class with Mr. Richards (not one of my favorite teachers) and we were talking about the appendix, and what appendicitis felt like. It all sounded so familiar! And it was nice to put a name to my previous experience.

"Oh, I had one of those!" I told the class—brightly, casually, as though saying, "Oh, yes, I've seen an ostrich. At the zoo."

Mr. Richards looked at me and said, "Did you have surgery?"

"No," I said. "It just went away."

Well. Mr. Richards, with whom I had butted heads quite a bit in the past, was certain that he had just caught me in a big, braggy lie. "You would be dead," he said, "if your appendix had burst and you didn't have it removed."

And, of course, I had to believe him. So I was completely embarrassed (at best) and humiliated (at worst). I figured he and everyone else must have thought that I was either stupidly mistaken or outright lying. On the other hand, I sincerely believed that there was no way in the world I could have had all those symptoms that he listed, without having had appendicitis.

So this became an unsolved mystery that I carried around and thought about and doubted and pondered my entire life. Had the eight-year-old me been simply wrong, to feel that my life was in danger? Had I overreacted? Or was I mis-remembering the whole event?

Now fast forward again, twelve years. I was twenty- six. I had been having a lot of pain when getting my periods, so my OB-GYN conducted some exploratory surgery--during which he noticed something very peculiar about my appendix!

He called it "roadkill."

He said it "almost looked like it had ruptured." In fact, he couldn't believe that it *hadn't* ruptured. But we supposedly know (because Mr. Richards had said so) that if it had, I would have been dead. Right?

Wrong.

I am here to tell you that, after every subsequent surgery I have had since then, doctors all say the same thing. They can't believe my appendix. They can't believe I went through whatever I went through, and am still alive and kicking.

I can't believe it either. But I'll tell you what I can believe: God heard the prayer of an eight-year-old little girl who did not want to die. He knew that, more than anything in this world, I wanted to live and become a Mommy. And so God answered my prayers that night.

True, He took His sweet time in letting me know. But He answered me.

A miracle? Yes. But it was only the first of many miracles in my life.

Chapter 2

My Snow Queen Dress

My Mother died at a very young age.

She was Italian, straight off the boat. She spoke seven languages and was one of the most beautiful women I have ever seen. (Am I being objective? No. She was my mother.) She died when she was twenty-three. (And I was four at the time.) I believe they called it an "accidental overdose"— possibly of a malaria medication. But it may have been from depression.

In any case, my father remarried when I was in the eighth grade. He married a woman with two children. She did not like me very much and, to be kind, that is all I am going to say about it.

When I was seven years old my father was a part of an organization called the JCCs. "Jewish Community Center"? I doubt it. Still, they were in charge of a lot of different things in our small community—one of which was the Snow Queen contest. I will never forget watching all those girls in their beautiful gowns, vying for the title of Miss (Name of Town, Which I Am Deliberately Omitting, Here).

My favorite girl wore an orange chiffon dress. Orange! Chiffon! And she won. A man came up to me after that ceremony and said, "When you get big, you're going to be the Snow Queen, too." And I believed him. (This wasn't as easy as it sounds.) I spent a good portion of my childhood being told I would amount to nothing. I always wondered if they thought they were motivating me or if they really meant what they said. I will blame it on liquid courage. So from that day on, I practiced my triumphant, regal, newly-crowned wave. I couldn't wait until my senior year so that I could go out for the title.

That meant waiting eleven years. Which I did.

Finally my senior year arrived. Life, however, wasn't what I had expected. I had left for the summer and worked at a resort, at which time I had learned exactly how stressed out I was living at home. Without going into much detail-- as my father has asked me for forgiveness and of course I gave it to him--the only thing I can say is I had a very troubled relationship with both my father and my stepmother.

I had spent a weekend babysitting and had come home on a Sunday night. I don't remember whether I remembered, as I arrived, that it was my stepsister's birthday—but I sure found out when I walked in the door. My stepsister had been celebrating, which—like so many things—had really lit my stepmother's fuse. My stepsister was drunk. My stepmother was drunk. And, of course, my father was drunk. I walked into a hornet's nest.

My stepmother took one look at me and told my father that I had mouthed off to her. Never mind that it wasn't true. When everybody's drunk, it doesn't matter what's true or not. My father, of course, believed it. Let's just say it wasn't pretty after that.

It went from being an uneventful weekend to an evening that would change my life! After finding myself at the bottom of the steps I resolved that would be the last experience that I would ever have like that again. I went to my room, grabbed some clothes, stuffed them under my shirt, and left the house in a dead run.

Where did I go? I ran to the police station. I reported what had happened, and asked an officer to take a drive with me. I asked him not to make me go home. I told him that if he made me go home I would surely end up killing myself.

He told me he wouldn't force me to go back. Now, what you have to understand is, my father was a very well-respected man in our community. So to understand this story, you really need to know how important it was that the police officer never made me return home. I would like to again say my father has been forgiven for all. He is now the father that I always wanted. (An answered prayer!)

I moved into an apartment. My landlord was a very nice lady who allowed me to pay $75 a month for rent. I was still in high school, of course, but managed to hold down three jobs: I was a waitress, I did babysitting, and I worked at a boutique.

That last fact would pay off, big, in about six weeks.

The Snow Queen contest was to be held a month and a half after I left home. My parents had not only gotten my stepsister a dress, they actually had had one *made* for her. I did not have a dress, nor really any money to buy one.

I went ahead and filled out the application. I worked at this project as though I were executing a job. I called around and spoke to other former Snow Queens and asked their advice. I wrote and rewrote my essay application. But, no matter how well all that went, the fact remained that I still had no dress. I went to bed one night and I prayed. I asked God, *Please, whatever you can do for me, please--I have twelve dollars and I need a dress really bad.*

Remember that third job? I had been working at the local boutique, and everything they sold was very expensive. There was also a flower shop in the basement, and I'd do deliveries for them around town. Now, the whole time I'd been working there, I had assumed that, to get from the basement to the first floor, you had to go outside, put up with whatever weather there was, and climb the (often slippery) outside stairs. Then, one day, I noticed that there was a door behind the flower shop desk. I asked where it went. They told me "upstairs." But the door was stuck closed, so no one ever used it.

Well I sure wanted to use it.

So I pried it open—it wasn't that hard—and noticed a corner of a piece of fabric, behind another door at the bottom of the staircase, just kind of hanging there. I pulled at it and it turned out to be--are you ready?--*a beautiful wedding dress.* It was just hanging on a hook on the back of the door.

I asked whose it was, and the answer was, a girl I worked with. It turned out that a bridal shop in an adjacent town had caught fire, so she had bought the dress (which at the time completely smelled of smoke) for a reasonable price, in what was literally a fire sale. That must have been a while ago, though, because the dress certainly didn't smell of smoke now.

I asked the girl if I could buy it from her, and if it would be alright if I paid for it over time. She laughed and said, "Sure. But you have to pay me exactly what I paid for it." I gulped and asked how much.

"Five dollars."

I was thrilled. The dress was perfect. Then the flower shop donated sixty yards of pink and white ribbon. I took the dress and the ribbon to a seamstress and asked (holding my breath) how much she would charge to sew it on and make bows.

"Seven bucks."

I will never forget looking in the mirror, truly feeling like Cinderella. I thought, I am going to the contest with a dress that literally came out of nowhere. Not only was it a dress, but it was the best dress.

When I went to the contest, I was a wreck. It had been a month and a half since I had moved out of my father's house, but I knew that my stepsister had also entered the contest, and that my parents would be in the audience. They would clap for her, of course—but would they clap for me? Or would they sit there and just kind of look the other way? Either seemed possible. (And how would I feel—really—if they did clap for me? Happy? Resentful? Would I burst into tears? And, if so, what kind of tears?) So I was in the grip of a very strange mood, both sad and excited at the same time.

We went through the machinations of the contest and finally it was time to announce the winners. They called the second runner-up. It wasn't me. They called the first runner-up. It wasn't me. They called the winner.

It was me.

What does it mean when we say "I can't believe it"? It means that the feelings in your heart haven't caught up (yet) with the knowledge in your head. Your brain knows something is true but your emotions haven't kicked in accordingly. That's how it was for the first few seconds. I had felt like a loser my whole life, and now God had shown me that I was a winner. I had dreamed of that day forever, and now I was finally able to try out the wave that I had practiced for so many years. (It was very effective.)

I pray that God shows you the winner in you, that you have your day to practice your wave, that your best dress falls from the sky, and that no matter how bad it hurts or how scared you are, you put that dress on, and let God show you the winner in you.

I feel compelled to write that forgiveness--a necessity in the role of a Christian--was very hard for me. I asked God over and over to help me forgive my father, especially after he had asked. (His asking came completely out of the blue, uncoerced, a truly heartfelt request.) I said yes, of course, then I hung up and I didn't feel any different. So I prayed and asked God, "How can I forgive him?" and He very clearly and simply replied, "Because it's easier to be you than him." And, truly, it is easier to forgive someone else than to forgive yourself. Ever since then, forgiveness has been very easy for me.

In regard to my stepmother, I had a very strange encounter with forgiveness with her. It came upon her death. I had no idea she was even sick. I never called home, but maybe once every four months, so it was normal for me not to know what was going on. (They even sold their house and moved cities once without telling me. I had to call around town to find out what happened to them.) So this was a normal for us, unfortunately. I was awakened at about three-thirty in the morning and it scared me. I reached across my husband for the phone, and that woke him. He asked me what I was doing.

I said, "The phone is going to ring. I'll take it downstairs." He sat up and looked at me and didn't say a word, just shook his head, meaning WHAT????? I went downstairs and waited for the phone to ring. It took about twenty minutes and sure enough, it rang. It was my brother, calling to tell me our stepmother had died.

I knew right there and then what had woke me up: It was her, and I knew she could see me. So when I hung up I spoke to her out loud and asked her if she could see my heart. I asked her if she could see that all I ever wanted was for her to love me like a daughter, and I wanted to love her like a mother. I hoped she could now see me and my heart and my true intentions. And all of a sudden I got this feeling of peace that came over me, like an acknowledgment of my sadness and a love from her that I had always longed for. Hence, then came forgiveness. I thank God for that freedom, through His peace and His gift of understanding. I am now free.

Chapter 3

Lauren's Birthday Cake

Growing up without a mother, I had plenty of challenges — especially when it came to learning how to be a *female*. If there was no one from whom I could learn such things in my home, I was forced to look elsewhere.

One place was at my aunt's house in North Dakota. My father would ship me there every summer, from when I was around six until around fifteen. Did I say "ship me there"? I meant "allow me to escape to." It was a pleasure to be in a normal home, and watch a nice woman go about her normal business. My aunt was an amazing woman, with the patience of a saint. She treated me like her own and was very, very good to me. I believed she loved me and I certainly loved her.

But it wasn't enough for me. When you grow up aware that you lack something, and you make it your business to obtain it, you do a more thorough job than others who just take it for granted. So I studied how to be a lady. What did I study? What else? Movies!

I loved the old, classic films on TCM, and took them all literally. I watched Irene Dunne and Claudette Colbert and Ginger Rogers and Gene Tierney swan around with Cary Grant and Jimmy Stewart and Clark Gable. I admired their gowns and dresses. I loved to watch them glide through those impossibly enormous apartments and townhouses under fabulous chandeliers amid sumptuous furniture. I studied their elegance, their manners, their posture and carriage and deportment.

But I didn't study how to be a Park Avenue swell, which — let's face it — I wasn't sure I'd ever have a chance to be. I also watched Tammy Faye and Jim Bakker on their religious broadcasts and learned, if nothing else, the awesome power of mascara. And my idea of perfection included the households on The Brady Bunch, Leave it to Beaver, and the mom-less but super-relaxed and comfy family consisting of Andy Taylor, Aunt Bea, and Opie on the Andy Griffith Show.

Those, to me, depicted what was normal. That, to me, looked like a great life. How great? Put it this way: when I needed a babysitter for my third kid, I prayed for — and got! — an Aunt Bea-type.

Because, as weird as it sounds, I really believed that life was like that in *everyone else's* house.

I think what I was really missing was tradition. When I was a Girl Scout, I would go to my leader's house and discovered that they had a tradition for everything. Same thing at my Aunts' houses--when they celebrated birthdays, they always had a beautiful cake, and balloons, and pretty napkins. Yes, I know — *more* girly things.

It almost goes without saying that I had always wanted a birthday party. In fact, when I was ten, I went to school and told everyone that I was having one. No, it wasn't true, but when you're ten, you somehow think that maybe it can be true. In this case, though, I remember being in the bathtub as the doorbell kept ringing. Finally my dad came in and said, "Did you tell everyone that you were having a birthday party?" I had to confess. He wasn't thrilled. He sent my friends home and I was heartbroken.

This, then, is an example of how your childhood experience forms the adult you become. I promised myself that when I had kids, they were going to have great Christmases, great birthdays with parties, and that we would celebrate everything as though it were a national holiday.

Fast forward to Tucson. Lauren my oldest child, was turning seven. And, as I had sworn years earlier, she had already had great birthday parties for each of the previous six years. This year, in the spirit of go-big-or-go-home, she wanted to invite her whole class of first grade girls to spend the night. There would be pizzas, soda, a dance party, and swimming. It would be, in seven-year-old terms, a blast.

Being a single mom, I had to plan everything out— especially the financial aspect of it. (I was putting myself through college at the time, and every dollar counted.) I had gotten everything taken care of: the pizza, the soda, the chips; I was making caramel rolls for breakfast and all the treats for in-between. And of course, the present.

Done and done! I was so proud of myself that I completely forgot a few not-so-little items.

On the morning of the party, my daughter reminded me of our tradition, in which the birthday child gets to go to every grocery store on earth, look at all the birthday cakes, and pick out the one she or he wants, no matter the cost. Oh, and there was another tradition I also had forgotten: It's your birthday? Then you get to decide where you want to eat, and you just get any darn thing you want off the menu.

These were things that I had not budgeted for. I had $12.10 left. That was it. No more, not a dime. (Trust me; I remember looking under my car floor mat for change that might have dropped.) I started stressing out. I said "Lauren, this year I thought we could make a cake and frost it ourselves. Won't that be fun!!?"

She wasn't having it. She looked at me and said, "No mommy, I really like when we go and look for the cakes."

So I said, "Let's go and see."

We went to the store that was closest to us and she found the cake of her dreams, right off the bat. It was white, with big purple flowers. By far the prettiest cake there, it came in at a, to me, whopping $14.95. I start sweating; I really wasn't sure what I was going to do. I said, "Let's go to another store and look! Maybe there'll be another one that's even better."

It's a measure of my desperation that I was delighted when she agreed. But my moment of relief was shattered when she said that she was hungry and wanted her birthday meal to be at Burger King.

Yes, it could have been worse. But I was beyond tapped out. I thought, "Oh my, Lord, please help me. I can't do this. Please! I do not want to let her down."

We went to the drive-through and I asked Lauren what she wanted. She said, "I want a cheeseburger and..." Then she looked at me, and I could see that *she* could see the stress in my face. "...and that's all mommy. That's all I want."

I knew--and she knew, and we both knew that we knew, that we just couldn't afford anything more. I was heartbroken.

When we pulled up to the window to pay and get our food, Lauren told the lady, "Today is my birthday!"

"It is?" The lady said. "Is there anything else you want?"

"Yes!" Lauren thought for all of one second and said, "I want a chocolate shake and french fries!"

"You do?" This angel said. "Well here you go!"

I went to pay, but the lady just smiled and said, "No, thanks. Have a great birthday!"

I was in complete shock. I was so happy! I just said, "Thank you, Lord. It is all You."

But I wasn't out of the woods yet. There was still the matter of the cake. I didn't know what to do. We went from store to store, trying to find a better (i.e., for me, cheaper) cake. But nothing else would do. Lauren kept saying, "Mommy, I want the cake with the purple flowers. I am the purple girl and my friend Monica is the pink girl."

So I drove back to the first store. I said a prayer before I went in. Then I walked up to the counter and asked them to write, *HAPPY BIRTHDAY PRINCESS LAUREN* on the white and purple cake.

While they were busy, I looked at the checkout, and looked at the lady behind the counter, writing out Lauren's birthday message, and I said, "Lord, You said faith could move a mountain. I need something that big. I need something to happen between here and the checkout. PLEASE!"

They finished inscribing the cake. (It looked wonderful.) I took it in my two hands, and began the long walk over to the checkout. I moved as slowly as humanly possible, on off chance that something miraculous would intervene. I looked around, thinking—well, hoping--that an alarm would go off, confetti would fall from the ceiling, and the manager would jump out in a tuxedo and announce that I was the one millionth customer—and that I'd won a free cake!

That didn't happen. Nothing remotely like that happened. I kept walking until I ran out of space and reached the checkout. I put the cake on the moving belt and the cashier rang it up.

"$4.35, please."

I can be very chatty. And I have a good sense of humor. So it's not often that I run out of things to say. But that was one occasion that I did. All I could manage was, "What?"

"$4.35 please."

I was in a state of shock. Inwardly, I asked why. God just said,"Be quiet. This is what you asked for."

I don't know how else to explain what happened that day. I just know that God not only answered my prayers, He answered all my needs and even sent me home with some money. Now, I'm not saying that a birthday cake and a burger, fries, and a shake are equal to any life crisis that you might have. As a matter of fact, I'm sure that you've had much greater needs than those. So have I. We all have.

However, what I'm here to tell you is, God is there for everything, not just the occasional gigantic crisis. He's there for small crises, too. He's at Burger King, and at the bakery department of your local supermarket. He is there to answer, not just every prayer, but every question. He is an amazing God! He created the world! So, obviously — and as I can testify — a birthday cake, or a fast-food meal are no big deal for Him. I learned, on that day, to go to Him for all things, big or small.

Oh, yeah — we had the party with first grade girls. It was wonderful.

Chapter 4

The Pinetop Trip

When I first met my husband, he looked like a wild boy.

I was twenty-three, living in Tucson and working in property management at a pretty ritzy apartment complex. Steve's mother called and asked if her boys could move in. All three of them were in college, so my immediate reaction was: No way.

We had a classy clientele. The last thing they or we needed was a unit full of college bros, throwing loud parties and strewing beer cans around the common areas. And we weren't the only ones. In fact it was legal for us to deny applications from college kids. But the mother was very persistent. She had her husband call the owner of my management company and convinced my boss to let the three boys move in. I took one look at their mother and thought, wow, she's so beautiful, classy, and very elegant, maybe this will work out.

I made them my neighbors so I could keep an eye on them (and so I wouldn't have to walk very far in my nightgown when I got the inevitable disturbance calls). And that's how I met Jeff and James, the 18-year-old twins...and 24-year-old Steve.

Now, what you have to understand is, I had been dating a lot at that time, and I was used to dating boys who were...let's say, Mr. Wall Street: Conventional, well-groomed young men in suits and ties, with office jobs and normal haircuts. I had also prayed a lot about who and what I had in mind.

Steve fit none of those specs. He had long hair, wore an earring, and played guitar in a band. He was no Mr. Wall Street. He was A Real Bad Boy.

So why had God sent him to me? I think because, although I may not have been aware of it, I was requesting someone with an amazing heart, who was genuine and compassionate — which I was unable to see, at first, having been put off by the hair, earring and rock band. In any case, we knew each other for three years before we ever dated. And when that began, he made it clear that he was an atheist. He didn't believe in God and I was not going to force him to. (He had been through a lot: His baby, with his first wife, had died shortly after childbirth, and his wife had never recovered. She eventually got lost to drugs and alcohol.)

I think he was a truly broken man. I prayed about him, saying, "Lord, if he is not the one, take him away and heal me quick!" (We've been married 23 years and I *still* pray for that. hehe) And he didn't go away: He was a college student and worked for a title company, but every night he came home to an apartment practically next door to mine. So I saw him all the time.

To this day I'm surprised at how he put up with me. For four months we didn't so much as kiss. Since the only TV I had was in my bedroom, when we sat in the living room I made him sit on one couch while I sat on the other. It's a good thing he didn't complain, because I had high standards. As far as I was concerned, I was a lottery ticket: there would be one winner only. He must have agreed with me, because he never pushed.

The bad news was that atheism thing. I prayed and prayed about it, but God just told me not to worry. Steve would not only be a Christian, but would become more of a man than I could ever imagine. He would exceed my expectations of what I wanted for my husband.

So one day he called and asked if I wanted to go to Pinetop, a little town up north, with woods and a lake. His parents had a cabin up there and we could enjoy a nice weekend. I thought it sounded like fun and said yes. At the end of work Friday we got in his car and started—

--except not quite. Just before we actually left the driveway, I said, "Pull over, I forgot to pray." He rolled his eyes and said no. I said, "Pull over so I can pray, or you can take me home."

He pulled over and said, *"Make it quick."*

I first asked God for his forgiveness. (I heard Steve sigh.) Then I asked God to bless our trip. (Steve squeezed my hand, meaning, *Hurry up.*) Finally I asked God to protect us on our trip, that we might be safe.

Steve let go my hand. I don't know whether he said, "Amen" when I did. Maybe he did.

We hit the road, on a trip that takes around four hours on a winding mountain road—often, of course, behind slowpokes who think they own the highway. Eventually all that winding back and forth acted like a hammock on me, and I fell asleep. I don't know how long I was out...

...but I do know that suddenly something woke me up: an ice-cold presence, something almost palpable. It physically shook me out of my nap, as though some invisible presence of evil were sitting right there. The whole atmosphere in the car changed. I started screaming, "The spirit of death is here! The spirit of death is here!"

Bear in mind that I had never heard of anything called "the spirit of death"—not in church, not in Scripture, not anywhere. So it's not as though that idea was already in my head, waiting to be activated by some vague sense of misgiving. No, this was out of nowhere and had me utterly terrified.

I told Steve to stop the car. He (quite understandably) started yelling, "What? What spirit of death?" When I finally realized what he was referring to—when it dawned on me that he was quoting *me*—I said I didn't know. I just insisted he pull over and stop. So he did. And I made him stay there for quite some time (it may have been minutes; it felt much longer) until the feeling went away.

He wasn't thrilled. In fact he called me a kook, and said the first chance he had to dump me once we got back home, he was going to do it. I didn't care. I just knew we couldn't proceed until the spirit of death went away. Eventually, it did, and we got back on the road.

Not five minutes later we came upon a grisly sight: two smashed cars, police and ambulance vehicles, and several dead bodies in body bags.

I thought I saw three. To this day, Steve swears there were two. But we both agreed that, had we kept on driving and not pulled over, we could have been involved in that disaster.

"Now you know why I pray, and why I believe," I told him.

He barely spoke. In fact he was shaken and quiet the whole weekend. We had a nice time, boating and enjoying the lake, but something profound had taken place to the two of us, and he knew it as much as I did. How do I know that? Because when we left to drive home, he pulled over and asked me to pray for a safe trip.

Oh, and shortly after that, I tried calling him to confirm some date we had arranged, and was puzzled why he didn't pick up. I found out later that he'd been busy doing something else. It turned out that a Methodist minister had been in the neighborhood, knocking on doors to share the Good News. Steve answered and, when the minister asked if he was a Christian, said no.

"Would you like to be?" the man asked.

Steve said yes.

No wonder he'd ignored the phone. He was busy with something more important.

Chapter 5

My Sabina

When I was twenty years old I found out I was going to be a mother.

The pregnancy may have been unplanned but was certainly not unwanted. And while I started out sad and scared, pretty soon those feelings were replaced by feelings of excitement. I thought for sure that life was going to be the fairy tale that I had always wanted.

Being young, I really did not know much about pregnancy, and I certainly hadn't read that much. So I thought my own pregnancy was proceeding normally. I went to my doctor's appointment every month, and all seemed to be fine, until one day (around my fifth month) they asked me to take the alpha-fetoprotein test. Of course I had no idea what that was for, but we had had no problems in our family (that I knew of), so I took the test and didn't think twice about it.

Some time passed, until one day I got a phone call, out of the blue, telling me "please call your doctor." I called.

The doctor asked why we had not called back for weeks. I said we had moved and were busy. She exclaimed, "You need to get in here right away. The blood test came back and your baby could be suffering from severe Down's Syndrome and be disfigured."

I was horrified. I loved my baby! Then the doctor went on to say, "You need to get in here right away so we can do another test. If it comes back positive you can abort." ABORT? My baby? It was unthinkable. I couldn't believe it. Thinking about it, I could barely *breathe*.

I went in the following day and took the other test. That was followed by ten long days of hell. I literally felt as though I was going to die of a broken heart. On the third day I started bleeding. I called the doctor and told her. She said, "Chances are, you're miscarrying."

I hung up the phone and asked God, "Please save my baby. *Please.*"

I bled for five days—and then the test results came back: My baby was going to be fine. That very day, the bleeding stopped! And when it was time, I gave birth to an 8-pound, 9 ounce baby girl named Lauren Ashley. She was the pride and joy of my life.

But I never quite got over that scare. Maybe it's like being in a car accident in which you don't get hurt. You know this kind of thing happens to other people, but assume they can never happen to you. Until it does.

Fast forward to nine years later. I was pregnant with my second child, and I had decided the day that I found out that I was pregnant, that I would *not* have that test done. It was way too stressful. I wanted to enjoy my pregnancy. Still, the memory of what I had gone through with Lauren still brought an ache, still haunted me. Even though I had made the decision not to have the test, I obsessed over it anyway! I thought about it every moment of every day and I had no peace at all. And, of course, peace was the one thing I wanted for this pregnancy since I hadn't had it with the last one.

I was about seven months pregnant and was in a grocery store with Lauren. I was walking up and down the aisles in a daze, with nothing in my cart. I was overwhelmed with worry. Was my baby ok? Should I have had the test? Was I jeopardizing the baby's health?

Lauren wanted doughnuts so I sent her to get some. And I stood by myself in some deserted row of the grocery store and I started crying. I said to God, "Lord, I can't do this anymore. I'm scared for my baby and I can't rest from worrying. So please, Lord, help me. I can't do this anymore."

I heard the Lord say, "Go over to the strawberries." I went over to the strawberries—and immediately saw something odd: They were being sold openly by the pound. In my experience strawberries had always been sold in plastic cartons, by the pint, covered in plastic wrap.

The Lord told me, "Now pick one up." I did. "Look at it," He said. "Look at all the details on the strawberry. Notice how it is connected with webbing all over it." Now, I don't know about you, but I had never really, *really* looked at a strawberry before. I was amazed at how complex it was—how intricately detailed. Then He told me to open one up. So I did. I broke the strawberry open and looked at its structure inside. I was amazed at how beautifully detailed it was. Then he told me to taste it. So I did.

It wasn't the sweetest strawberry in the world, but it *was* a strawberry. Then the Lord told me to look at all the other strawberries and to notice how they all looked different, but how they were all still webbed, and how they all had different shapes but *they were all still strawberries*. Some were sweeter than others. Some were bigger than others. Some were more red than others. In fact, no two were alike. But they were all strawberries.

He reminded me that He had made each and every one of those strawberries. He had devoted His time and His attention to creating them--and that He had taken even more time and devoted even more attention to creating my baby. He said that she was going to be just fine.

I finished eating that strawberry and burst into tears. I stood there weeping in the Produce Section and hoped no one was watching. And I asked God for his forgiveness. Soon after that I realized He must have forgiven me, because Sydney Sabina was born two weeks early and weighed 8.4 pounds and was perfect from head to toe!

Chapter 6

Tom

Growing up the way I did, I didn't have that much faith in people. And I probably had even less in myself. Because remember: Your parents are the first people who tell you what you are. And, since they're right about so many things (how the stove works, and how to drive a car) and they provide you with so many things (food, clothes, all that) you end up believing them about just about everything. Plus, of course, you need them in order to survive. So you just figure that *they know*.

And when your father and stepmother constantly tell you you're bad, and wrong, and a problem, you believe it—at least at first. You also start to assume the rest of the world thinks that way of you, too.

So I always was very nervous and worried about what was coming next. I would say that, even after I'd grown up and moved out of my parents' house into the world, I kind of felt like a target. And yet, the weird thing was, everyone was always sure, for some reason, that life was easy for me.

Why? Well—and I'm trying to say this with sincere modesty—I've always been blessed in the looks department. When you're what most people think of as being attractive, people think you've got it made. You have (people think), no trouble finding sex, or love, or getting hired for jobs, or being welcomed into whatever group or club or organization or clique you'd care to join.

So there I was: constantly fearing the worst from people who thought I was happy as a clam. Because I was so nervous, it was easy to pick on me--especially at work. I was always very nervous about losing my job, so I compensated like crazy and tried my hardest to overachieve. I had worked for some great people who had taught me some great work ethics. Still, I never felt quite up to par.

I'd been fired from a job that I actually liked, at a real-estate office. I was hired to take the place of a woman who did not know she was getting fired. She was to train me and then they were going to let her go. Well, either because of my nervousness I let something slip, or she just sensed what was going on. In any case, she saw what was coming, and started sabotaging me. The result was, the person who got let go was me.

Now, being fired was my worst fear. How could it not be? When you just "know" there's something wrong with you, you live in fear of others finding it out. So when I got sacked, I couldn't just roll with it, or chalk it up to experience, or decide it was for the best. I took it hard. I just went home, and lay down, and prayed. I asked God, "Please, Lord, bring me a job, one that I can learn from and grow in." It was a terrible day and a rough night.

In the morning my boyfriend, Steve (he's now my husband) asked me what I was going to do — and when I said, "I don't know, something will happen," he very kindly reminded me that he couldn't support me! ("Thanks, sweetie.") He left and I lay on the couch. No TV, no radio. Just me talking to God.

I said, "What now, Lord?" I got no reply — or so I thought. Then, after a few lonely hours, the phone rang. It was a man named Tom, whom I had interviewed with *two years* before. He asked, "Would you be interested in being a manager for me? At one of the properties that I oversee?"

I thought hard about it for at least a third of a second. Then — duh--I said yes and asked when he needed me to start. He said right away. I said, "Is Monday good?"

Monday was good. In fact Monday was great. He paid me more than I had ever earned before. And even though, as you know, I have complete faith in God, still: I couldn't believe it.

The work started. It was a completely dilapidated property; people were running drugs through it and about 25% of the tenants were not paying their rent. In other words, I had no idea what I was in for. It took me months to clean that place up. I turned about 70% of the apartments and handed out the most eviction notices that I had ever done. I was harassed and threatened; I had tenants threaten to kill me. It was crazy. Meanwhile, as all of this was going on, my corporate office was all over me, demanding reports that I'd never heard of. I was staying till all hours of the night.

One day Tom, my boss, walked in, all six-feet-four of him. (Have I mentioned that he looked like Tom Cruise?) He took one look at me, sat down in a chair next to mine, and asked what was wrong. I told him that I was getting very little sleep, trying to get the property turned around and collect all the rents *and* get these crazy reports done.

"What reports?" he asked.

"All these reports Betty ordered up," I said.

He asked me to show him. When I did, he said — well, I'm not comfortable writing what he said. Let's just say, he was from New York, and he expressed himself in colorful language. If you know what I mean and I think that you do.

Tom said, "Why would you allow someone to treat you like this?"

"I thought it was my job," I said.

"No," he said. "She's harassing you. Why wouldn't you call me?"

Again, all I could say was that I thought it was part of my job. He looked at me and said, "Child, do you have a father?"

Tom was in his sixties and I was in my twenties. It seemed okay for him to call me "child." I said yes, I do have a father. "Do you have a good relationship with him?"

"No. Not really."

He stood up and said, "Child, no one has a right to be mean to you. You command respect." He told me that, from that point on, he would write me up if I let anyone push me around. He looked at me and said, "Now I know why God sent you to me. You need a Father. You poor child."

Tom taught me a lot about life. He taught me how to always understand that everything I did affected someone else's life. *Everything.* When I had to fire someone, I first had to make sure that I had given them every chance to redeem themselves. And he made me believe in *me.*

Three years after I'd started working there, Tom was diagnosed with a liver disease. He needed a transplant. On top of that, Tom's wife of thirty years was leaving him. (Talk about when it rains it pours.)

We spent a lot of time talking about the Bible and how God works. It was an amazingly tough time for him—but he went on to have his transplant (literally within twenty four hours of dying), and eventually healed, both from the ailing liver and the broken heart. Meanwhile, the property I had been working at was sold, so I would not work with him anymore.

Over the next few years we would get together and go to Bingo night or to dinner. We would just talk about God; I remember praying with him for a wife. And then, after a few years had gone by, Tom met Lori. I was so excited! He was in love!

But after a while I realized that I hadn't heard from him in some time. This man who called me the daughter he never had--had he abandoned me? I was heartbroken. I would call and leave messages, but he never called back. This went on for years, but still I heard nothing. I had known that his second wife hadn't liked me, so maybe that accounted for it. Maybe she thought I was a threat to her relationship. That would have been absurd, but sometimes there's no understanding people.

Then, one night, I had a dream--a very strange dream. I know all dreams are strange, but with most dreams, you wake up the next day and just laugh and think, "Huh." Not this time. With this one I woke up the next day and thought, "Oh, no..."

Tom was in it. He and I were laughing--but something was different. It wasn't like *we* were "really" dancing. It was like our souls were dancing, and laughing, too. All of a sudden, in the dream, I started crying and saying "No..." Tom told me he was dying.

When I woke up in the morning I was immediately scared. I tried to call Tom's cell but it had been disconnected. I thought, it was only a dream! Don't worry about it!" Besides, it was Christmas Eve and I had lots to do.

Around mid-day I realized that I had not bought a tie for my youngest son. So I ran over to a department store that I never go into. And boom: inside I ran into Jack and Lucille. They had been Tom's friends for thirty years. I thought, "This is great! I can tell them about my dream and they can tell me he's okay!" I asked them how Tom was and voila! They said he was doing great!

I laughed with relief. I said, "Thank God! I had a dream last night and I dreamt that he was dying. In the dream he was saying goodbye to me." I added, "--and you know what they say about those kinds of dreams."

They looked at me, and laughed, and said, "Oh, yes, Tom is fine." So we started talking about other things--their children, my children, the weather...Finally I said, "It's getting late, and we have to get over to our in-laws. It was great to see you — "

That's when Jack's expression changed completely. He grabbed my arm and said, "Listen, there is something you need to know. Tom's wife, Lori, left him, and Tom is very sick. He doesn't want anyone to know. He's in hospice."

I asked what happened. He explained: Tom had fallen and broken his neck — or, at least, received some neck injury he wasn't aware of. When he finally went into a hospital, he contracted an infection that shut down his kidneys. It was classic hospital cascade, one thing after another.

I went home that night and wrote Tom a letter. I told him how he was my hero; how he had taught me to champion life; and how he had been many people's champion. Now, I said, I wanted him to champion — to beat--this illness. I sent him a Christmas picture of the kids and mailed it to his ex-wife.

I got a call from Barbara saying Tom wanted to see me. I was very glad. However, by then I had gotten a pretty bad cold, so I wasn't able to go right away. (The last thing I wanted to do was expose Tom to more problems.) Barbara called a few days later and said to come right away, that he didn't have much longer. Not much longer!

I had been thinking he had a year--not *days*. I called my husband and had him come home from work, then went straight to the hospice. I walked in and I tell you--this place just smelled of death. It struck me that I was not prepared to see him. And when I did, I realized I had been right.

He was a shell of who and what he used to be. This great big, 6'4" man who walked (and talked) like a mobster--we used to call him by a fake mobster name. He was The Preacher...I couldn't believe it. Where was my giant man? He was so weak, he would open his eyes only for a moment, and I thought: am I ever going to hear him speak again? So I sat there for a while and I tried to talk.

But it all felt so fake. I thought: I don't want it to be this way. This needs to be real.

Why? Because it seems to me, that in the presence of death, people feel bound by a sort of protocol: to deny what's going on, to put on a cheery front, to pretend to make plans for "next week" or "when you're out of here." I mean it makes some sense. We all know we're going to die and we all pretend we either don't know that or that it's not "really" going to happen. So we get paralyzed with empty politeness, or we create a kind of communal denial.

But if Tom had taught me anything, it was the value of my actual behavior, the effect it had on others. I knew he would want that lesson applied here, of all places. So I grabbed his face and I said, "Tom. Tom, open your eyes. Tom, I know there's a swear word in there somewhere!"

He opened his eyes and he said--

Okay, again, I can't quite write what he said. And I saw a momentary sparkle in his eyes. That was all I needed.

Meanwhile, his two sons, Chris and Scott, were there. They were great kids. (I say "kids," but we were about the same age!) They led a more fun, rock-and-roll sort of life than I did, but okay, fine. I stayed till about ten o'clock, and then I needed to get home and nurse my baby to sleep. I told them I would be back first thing in the morning.

I went home that night and I prayed, "Lord, why is he suffering so? He is such a good man. I don't understand this."

God told me, "He is afraid to die."

I had thought Tom had never been afraid to die. But the Lord told me to take my Bible the next day and read Tom the part in Revelations where it describes heaven, to remind him of where he was going. I thought, Well, I can do that, but I think his kids are going to think I'm crazy. I woke the next morning and remembered another thing that Tom and I had talked about: He had said if he knew he was dying, he would want everyone to toast his life. I had gotten a bottle of Dom Perignon from my mother-in-law for Christmas, and I thought what a great toast that would be. So I put both--the bottle of Dom Perignon, and my Bible— in my bag, and went back.

I walked in and there were his sons with all their friends. I thought, Man, this is going to be embarrassing. But one thing that I have learned is, when God tells you to do something, you do it. So I hemmed and hawed for a while, until finally I said, "I was talking to God last night and he asked that I read this part in the Bible to your Dad and remind him of where he's going." And they both said "sure"--they were going to have a smoke anyway, so it would be a great time for me to do that!

One of their friends stayed with me. I was a bit uncomfortable but I pressed on. I read to Tom about the beautiful pearl gates and the streets lined in gold. I held his hand, and I thought, *Can he hear me?* He hadn't said a word since the previous morning. I read to him...and then the song "Amazing Love" came to me. Now, I'm no singer. But I felt in my heart that he needed to hear it. So I sang that song to him. I was holding his hand—

--and suddenly he started to squeeze mine. He heard me. So I took that time to tell him how much I loved him and how he had changed my life. I also told him—because, as I said, I wanted this to be real, and not just bedside-polite—that even though he'd blown me off for years, *I* was one of the few who showed up now. He would have expected that from me, and so would I. And here I was.

Later, when his boys and their friends came back in, I pulled out the bottle of Dom and we toasted his life. I put some on a sponge for Tom.

He died the next morning.

At the memorial, I felt so many different feelings. I thought, *I wonder if he is here.* And I also thought about reading him the Bible, and if his kids had thought that I was weird. No one had said anything like that, but as I said earlier: Sometimes I didn't have much faith in people.

Tom's sister sat close to me while she was talking to a friend of his, and what I overheard her saying astonished me. She said Tom had been very afraid of dying. I interrupted her and asked, "How do you know that?" She said that Tom had told the Minister that a week before he died.

Thank God, I had listened. Even in his death, Tom was still teaching me.

I need you to hear me when I say, Please. Talk to God, and when He speaks to you, listen. It is not you, it is Him. He will guide you always.

Chapter 7

The Chandelier

When I was about six or seven years old I kept waking up from a certain dream. This dream had no people in it. It was just this house; I kept walking through the house every night. It was so amazing. There were giant pillars, chandeliers everywhere, and long hallways and a staircase that could only belong in a castle. It was obviously nothing that I had ever seen before in real life (although maybe in a movie or on TV).

I remember waking up every morning and going downstairs and asking my dad, "Whose house is this?" I would tell him every morning about this house and how amazing it was. And I can remember the very puzzled look on my dad's face, and his usual reply: "You're just dreaming!" Finally, I walked through the house one last time (in my dream) and looked in a mirror and said, "This is *my* house!" I woke up, so excited, and ran downstairs and told my Dad, "I found out whose house it is. It's mine!!"

My father sat me down and told me I would have to have lots of money for a house like that, and that most people don't have those kinds of homes.

Well, I have spent the better part of my life trying to create this house. I have purchased doors and windows and sinks and toilets, one at a time, paying cash all the way. I would save money, then buy another piece, and start over again — save, then buy; save, then buy. And by the way, these are not your average home decoration pieces; they're all very unusual and hard to find. I've had people look at me like I'm crazy.

As a matter of fact, they almost always *call* me crazy. And they all ask the same questions: *Do you have an architect? Do you have land? Where is it going to be located? And, of course, How can a girl who does not have millions possibly build a house like that?*

And it's true, I don't have millions. What I do have are two storage units (big ones) and a garage packed with the treasures for this house.

At one point my husband and I had sixty thousand dollars saved in the bank. I was sure I was closer than ever to my house. We both worked for the same company, a major regional bank. He went to the office but I was able to work from home. I ran ads for our services (in the Yellow Pages, for example), and routed calls to my home phone. When I signed to buy the ads, the company signed behind me, so I had no worries about how the ads would be paid for.

And I was loving life. I got to stay home with my kids and work at the same time. What could be better? I did that for about ten years. During the last year, things were going so great that I decided to take out three ads…

Yeah, things were great—until, on a hot evening in August, I had just put the baby down for the evening when the phone rang. It was my girlfriend--calling and *screaming* at me, "I thought you would tell me if something was going to happen!"

I had no idea what she was talking about. I said, "What? Is your husband cheating on you? I didn't know—"

"No! My husband's not cheating! The company went bankrupt!"

It had. This was in 2007, at the start of the big financial meltdown. Our bank was one of the first casualties. Now we were all out of jobs and we weren't going to get our last paychecks or any of our reimbursement money. Worse, the company hadn't signed behind me on the latest three ads. I was on the hook for them, to the tune of $96,000.

Needless to say, the next three years were horrible. I was sued personally for payment for the ads. My credit went into the toilet. Every dime we had saved went to pay off those lawsuits.

(In fact, we're *still* trying to recover from that.)

Now what? No money, no great job, the market upside down. We owed more on our house than it was worth. And, for the first time ever, I could not see how my house—quite literally my dream house!—was ever going to get built. And sure, that was the least of our problems. Still, I spent the next few years being bitter and resigned to the fact that I would never get it.

Then, one day, I had to go to our storage unit. I was having a graduation party for Lauren and I needed some material, and I could not spend one dime over my budget. I had not been in the unit since the fall of the empire (as I so fondly called it). I crawled up and over and through all the tons of stuff we had crammed in there, looking for a bag of fabric that I knew was in the back. The whole thing turned into a scavenger hunt.

All of a sudden I heard the Lord speak to me. "Stop," He said. "Look around. Your home is here. You have not lost it. Your dream is alive." So I did. I looked around, and saw one thing after another that I had acquired and that I still loved. It was as though I were shopping in my own storage unit. Suddenly I started laughing and giggling. And I said, "It *is* here. It will happen! But when?" I went home in a good mood for the first time in a long time.

Cut to six months later, in October. Lauren had moved out in August and had met a wonderful boy. His name was Ryan. She brought him home, and the minute I saw him, I knew he was going to be my son-in-law. We had a great weekend together. Lauren went home and called me the next day. She told me that, on the way back home, Ryan had said he would really like to marry her. Now, despite my knowing this was going to happen all along, I was in shock. She said, "It won't be for a few years, Mom, but you better get your house built!" I thought: *We have no money, and I don't see how we are going to get any!*

Then I had a great thought. *Well, my husband's family has what my children call a "castle." Maybe Lauren can get married there if my house isn't built by then.*

And so naturally, that very second the phone rang, and it was my mother-in-law. I told her that Lauren had just called, and that she and Ryan wanted to get married. I said, "If my house isn't built by then, can Lauren get married at your house?" My mother-in-law knew our financial situation, and how stressed out we were and my talking about getting the "house" flipped her switch. "Are you crazy?" she said. "You're not going to have your house anytime soon! You can barely make it month to month! She was right and I knew it!

Now, normally, she is a wonderful woman, and extremely loving and generous. It's just that my bringing up my dream house in the midst of our financial difficulties upset her. And it was true that we were barely making it month-to-month. Still, when I hung up the phone, I was enraged. I looked up and said, "God, am I crazy? Am I? I'm down here looking like Noah, building some ark that no one can see. I can't even afford the *chandelier* in this house that You say I'm going to have." I said, "Lord, a chandelier that belongs in this house would be about a hundred thousand dollars, and I don't have A HUNDRED DOLLARS. So what are You going to do? ARE YOU GOING TO *GIVE* ME A HUNDRED-THOUSAND-DOLLAR CHANDELIER?"

My bitterness set back in. I didn't smile for days. And bear in mind, this was not a materialistic thing. I'm not a greedy person. This was about a vision that I had been given and that now I couldn't figure out how to achieve. No matter how hard I tried to shake it, it kept coming back.

A few days later my girlfriend Robin called and asked me to look up an antique French painting for her on eBay. I said I would, but I didn't get around to it. Robin kept calling and reminding me, so finally I did it.

But when I got on eBay I realized I'd forgotten where to look, so I put 'French antiques' in the search field. I was browsing through three pages, looking for this painting, and up came these two chandeliers. They were the most beautiful chandeliers I had ever seen. They were eleven feet tall and seven and a half feet wide. The ball on the end of them was as big as a soccer ball. They were dripping with crystals as big as my hand. The opening bid was $4,000.00.

I couldn't believe it. Mind you, I didn't have $4,000.00, and I knew these weren't going to go for anything close to that. They were solid bronze antique chandeliers, imported from France in the late 20's early 30's. And, of course, they were being sold as a set. From the research I had done, I knew they were worth much more than $100,000.00 each.

I called Robin and told her to look at the chandeliers.

"They're amazing!" she said.

"I know."

"I want one!"

"So do I. But there's no way in the world these are going for anywhere near four thousand dollars—and, oh, by the way, I don't have any money."

"Well," she said. "Let's just call the guy to see what he thinks."

So we emailed him, he called me, and we set up a conference call with the three of us. His name was Charlie. He told us that he had been contacted by antique dealers and auctioneers--by twenty other people--and that the chandeliers were going to go for some big money. How did we react? We asked him if he would stop the auction and sell them to us for the starting price!

He said, "Maybe I didn't make myself clear. These are going to go for some big money. So no, I'm not stopping the auction."

We ended the call. Then Robin said, "I really want these!" I said I did, too. She said, "Let's call him back!" So we called him back and she asked him a great question: How did he intend to get those two giant, massive glass objects down from where they were hanging? (Robin knows a lot about construction and knew what questions to ask.) He told us they were twenty-eight feet in the air. We talked to him for another hour. Then she had her husband call and talk to him some more about getting them down.

I heard God say something from Romans 4:17. God is He "who quickeneth the dead, and calleth those things which be not as though they were." Meaning, God brings things into existence that didn't exist before.

So I sat down and said a very sincere prayer. I said to God that if He wanted me to have the chandelier, could He please one, make it happen, and two, please provide the money.

Nothing happened until the day the auction was to close. It was then that I got a call about one of my hard money loans. I used to arrange deals between investors and home buyers and would get a fee for putting them together. It turned out that one of them had just come through — and been funded for $2,000.00.

I thought, Well, there's *my* half! And I knew Robin had hers. Still, I also knew that these beauties weren't going to go for a measly 4K, so I more or less gave up. Robin called. She was very upset. She wanted that chandelier so bad! All I could tell her was that I had given it up, and to let me know how the auction went, because I just couldn't bare to watch it tick away on the computer.

Then, about half an hour before the end of the auction, the phone rang. It was Charlie. He said, "Mama, if you want these for four thousand, I'll stop the auction. I can't have just anyone up there taking these down. Someone could get hurt."

I cried for three days. It wasn't just from joy, for getting the chandelier. I felt humbled. I learned--*again*, since I already knew it--that your visions are from God. He supplies the way. I am not in control of this. As a matter of fact, I have probably been in the way. Give it over. All of it. Surrender. It is His turn to steer. What I realized that day was: the house will happen, in His time, not mine.

P.S. Two months later I was at my girlfriend's house and had fallen asleep while watching our children play-- something I never, ever do. So she got up and started looking on the computer, and found three matching chandeliers that were five and a half feet long—perfect for going down the staircase. I got them! I paid next to nothing for all three. Again, what a blessing!!

Chapter 8

Sue

I had just started working with a mortgage bank. I had been selling homes for years and had learned how to do the financing, so I was hired to start the manufactured home division for a very large mortgage company. The day I started was exactly one day after I found out I was almost three months pregnant. (It was with my first son, Blake, who was my third child).

Sue was our smiling receptionist, stationed just outside of my office. She was very helpful and very cheerful and seemed really genuine. I'm not sure why I liked her so much--we did not have that much in common; I was married and on my third child, while she was 41 and never married, with no children—but I did. (I say she had no children, but a few weeks after I met her, God gave me a word that she would in fact be a mother.)

Sue had been dating her boyfriend for just over a year, and seemed crazy about him. He also worked for the company, in our corporate office. I loved to listen to her talk about how much fun they had, holding hands, dancing, laughing like loons--wow, what a great guy!

Meanwhile, Marilynn was my husband's receptionist. I loved her, too. She was fifty-something but had the spirit of a twenty-something girl — and also, it must be said, a figure to match. Marilynn had been working for the company for years and my husband and brother-in-law adored her. She had been dating *her* boyfriend for about two years and was, yes, crazy about him. I loved to hear the stories she told after one of their weekends. They were wild, wild, wild — drinking, laughing, and even dancing on a table.

I didn't know who had a better boyfriend, Sue or Marilynn, but I was happy for them both.

After one particularly amazing weekend, Marilynn said, "I have never been with a man that makes me feel so free! I laugh until I cry." I smiled and thought, *What a great feeling*.

Then I went out to talk to Sue. She had just hung up the phone with her boyfriend, and was giggling. She said, "You know, I have never met anyone who makes me feel so free. We drink and laugh and dance on the table!"

What?

I asked Sue what her boyfriend's name was. Fearing the worst, I said, "Is it Kevin?" It was. So I went back into my office and called my husband. I asked him to take Marilynn out to lunch and ask her some questions about her boyfriend--whose name, I knew, was Kevin. I would take Sue out and ask *her* some similar questions. You can see what I suspected: That they were dating the same guy.

And they were. That scoundrel. That creep!

I felt that we had to tell them. And we did. Both Sue and Marilynn were broken-hearted. I felt like the Grim Reaper of love.

And that was pretty much the beginning of the end for Sue.

She started coming to work smelling of alcohol, glassy-eyed and stumbling. I would say, "Sue, were you drinking last night? Why? You still smell--go quick and brush your teeth, before you get into trouble." Over the next several months it happened a bit more frequently. I would ask if she had been drinking at night, and she would say no. But she'd come to work and be all bruised up, from falling. We would go to lunch together almost every day. I would ask her what was going on but she would assure me that everything was alright. Then, on days I didn't go to lunch with her, I started to notice that she was coming back from lunch with booze on her breath. I asked her, "Are you drinking?" but she swore on our friendship she was not.

Meanwhile, the office was buzzing with rumors: *Sue was a drunk.* I was furious. I stuck up for her and told them all that they were wrong. Then one day Andrew, one of the loan officers, told me that Sue had been struggling for years. She had had an addiction to alcohol for years. I went to her and asked her one more time, and one more time she lied to me.

I was sad and mad at the same time. "I can deal with you needing help," I said. "But I can't deal with the lies." I was so angry with her that I stopped speaking to her. I would not even look at her. I thought, *You made a fool out of me. I trusted you and stood by you and you lied to me. I now look like not only a fool, but an idiot.*

Sue was eventually laid off by our company. After she left, she wrote me letters, but I never answered them.

Then God started to speak to me about her. He explained that her pain was unbearable. She had no friends and hated life. He said that the key to her unhappiness was that she had never known love. But I was still mad! I didn't care. She had humiliated me, and I had no room for understanding.

Six months passed, during which I had not received a single letter from her. Then one day, out of the blue, I received a letter that said, "I can't believe you were right, I'm going to be a Mother!" She told me that she missed me and that she was sorry. But I still didn't reply.

What on earth was so wrong with me? Looking back today, I can't believe that I wouldn't even soften over a baby! But at the time, that's how I felt. There was no way I was going to let her back in.

A few months after her baby was born she called me—and immediately, I could tell that she was drunk. I thought, *She should never have gotten pregnant. That poor baby!* I didn't care if I never heard from her again. As a matter of fact, I *hoped* to never hear from her again.

But then...

A few more months went by, and I was sitting on the living room floor, and I clearly heard the Lord say, "You need to take a hundred and fifty dollars and send it to Sue. Write a note and tell her that God loves her. Nothing else."

So what did I do? I argued with God! I said, "I am NOT going to send that drunk a dime!" A few more days went by, and God said, "I need you to send Sue a hundred and fifty dollars, with a note that tells her that I love her!"

"NO," I said. "I AM NOT SENDING THAT DRUNK A DIME!"

God said, "You are my child and so is she. She needs your help."

"NO!"

I did not hear from God again about her. Pretty good, huh? I argued with God and I won.

Or so I thought.

A few weeks went by—and suddenly, all my loans started falling apart. I was baffled. I wondered, *What is this? Why is all my business going away?* And I instantly knew the answer. I knew that if I didn't send the money to Sue, there would be no more blessings given to *me*.

I grabbed a card and wrote "GOD LOVES YOU" and I put $150 cash and the card in the mail. If you want to know the truth, I didn't do it happily or willingly. I did it begrudgingly. I did it for selfish reasons. I was like a child cut off from her trust fund, who's been told by her daddy to shape up. I did it because I had to, not because I wanted to.

Eight months passed. I had not heard a word from Sue--but then, what did I expect? I had sent the money anonymously, after all. So, fine.

Then, early one morning, the phone rang. It was Sue. She said, "Can I talk to you, please?"

Still mad, still wary, I said, "I only have a few moments. Go ahead."

She started off by telling me how sorry she was for lying to me, and how sorry she was that she had hurt me. She explained to me that her life was awful. I silently listened as she explained her pain. Then she told me something that changed my life.

She explained that she had hit rock bottom. She did not know how she was going to feed her baby and buy diapers.

She was desperate and broke—and so she had made a heartfelt plea to God for help. Then she said, "You'll never believe it, but out of the blue I received a card in the mail with a hundred fifty dollars! And all it said was, 'God loves you.'"

She couldn't believe it. She said it changed her life. It showed her that there really *is* a God. She was now getting counseling, and had gotten on a therapeutic medication to help with her depression. Life was changing for her. I told her I was proud of her and that I would call her back, but I had to go.

I hung up and dropped to my knees. I asked God to please forgive me. I just could not believe how selfish I had been, and how unforgiving I was. God knew her need was coming, and He also knew I would be stubborn. What would have happened if I had not listened to him?

I thought, *God asks you for less than 1% of what you ask for.* That day changed *my* life. I know that God could have used anyone, but he chose me, because he knew I needed to understand forgiveness and to understand healing. I also learned that miracles and blessings go in both directions. God uses all of us to deliver them–if only we're open to it. I count Sue as a dear friend to this day! She will only know it was me that sent the money via God when she reads my book!

to repeat myself twice as much with you as with anyone else, in any of my classes, ever!" So I got the message.

It took about two weeks to set up the testing, and when the time came the teacher had me tested for everything under the sun. And get this: she was right. It turned out I had an auditory reception problem. *I heard only two to three words out if every five words that were spoken.*

How had I managed to get through high school? How was I going to get through college? So I came up with a plan: I resolved to read as much as I could, and asked others to make carbon copies of their notes for me. And it worked! I went from being an average student to being a great student. My confidence soared and I couldn't wait to get up every morning and go to school.

I had another overwhelming experience at college — the experience of having my professors try to ruin everyone's belief in God. It always amazed me when they would try to make me feel that I was actually dumb for believing in God.

The first minutes of my Philosophy class went like this: The professor asked, "Which one of you idiots believes in the story of Adam and Eve? Raise your hand." Apparently I was the only idiot in class who did, because when my hand went up it was the only one. He said, "You believe in God?"

I said, "Yes, of course I do!"

He said, "Prove to me that there is a God." So I started out with my explanation. But he shut me down with, "If you have to prove that there is a God, then there isn't one. If you have to prove something is real, that means it isn't real."

I personally thought that was the dumbest logic in the world. But I really couldn't argue with him. He had obviously had this discussion a thousand times and had rehearsed every comeback possible. So he was going to win, if only for the moment. However, at the end of our argument he said, "If you can prove to me, by the end of the semester, that there is a God, then I'll give you an A."

I said, "It's a deal!"

I was happy to hear it, although I'm pretty sure he only made that deal for two reasons: 1) He had done quite a number on humiliating me already. 2) He was very sure I wasn't going to be able to do it.

So what did I do? What else--I prayed and asked God to help me.

Meanwhile, my favorite class was Psychology. I had a great instructor. I learned so much--I couldn't believe all the things that I had not known growing up. The best thing I learned in that class was this tiny fact: Did you know that scientists have never pinpointed exactly *where* your mind is? They know your mind is somewhere in your head, but they really can't tell you where it is or how it works!

So, back to the atheist philosophy professor. It was nearing the end of the semester and I had yet to prove that God existed. The professor, meanwhile, had done a great job trashing God and running Him into the ground. One day he said, "How many of you believe that your mind can heal you?" Everyone raised their hand but me. He said, "What is with you? Everyone knows that your mind can heal you!"

I said, "Really? But where *is* your mind?"

"In your brain," he said.

"Really? Where in your brain?"

"IN YOUR BRAIN!"

"I heard you the first time," I said. "I asked you to pinpoint exactly where in your brain your mind is. And I would like it backed up with some scientific evidence."

He said, "You know that you have a mind. *Everyone* knows that you have a mind."

So I said, "Let me understand this. You expect me to believe that there is a mind somewhere in the brain, even though scientists and researchers cannot find it? And cannot prove that it is there? But even so, just because 'everyone knows that it's there,' I should believe you?"

He gave a great big grin and said, "Yes."

And then I said, "Touché! WHAT DOES THIS MEAN? It means that, if you can say the mind exists even if you can't prove it, then I can say there is a God even though I can't prove it. And by the way--God created it that way!"

That was the best A I ever earned.

Two years later I ran into my language professor in the bathroom. I giggled when I saw her. I asked if she remembered me, and she did. I thanked her for changing my life. She thought it was no big deal. I laughed and asked her to guess how many teachers I had had in my life--and none of them had been able to pick up my hearing disability that she had been able to figure out in three weeks. I thanked her for caring, and for being my College Angel that God had blessed me with.

(While writing this book I began hoping there was also a spelling angel out there. Although maybe that's why God gave us spellcheck.)

Life is going to try to throw you off of the path of what you know. As adults, we are taught to believe that only what we see is real, and that everything else is childish. It is *not true*. I encourage all of you: Believe to receive. You'll get all God's blessings. It is a blessing to be loved by Him. It is amazing. His loves heals all.

Chapter 10

Angels in My Bedroom

This chapter...

I'm not really sure how you're going to take this one. It's strange at best, and definitely the most mind-blowing and supernatural experience I have ever had. Some things you can explain away — but trust me. Not this. I've tried!

It happened on a midsummer night. The air was hot and — well, something from that Meatloaf song. I've always wanted to say (or write) that. Anyway, there was nothing special about this time in my life. Maybe I was in prayer more than usual, really praying for people more than I normally did. But in general life was pretty typical and uneventful. I didn't really need any extra weird events (as though I haven't had enough in my life) to make my week or year more interesting.

So. One night I went to bed early and watched a movie with my husband. The movie wasn't scary, so I have no idea where all this came from, but I knew almost instantly that this was not going to be an average night. I just had an

83

inner sensation, an intuition, an instinct. It's happened before, and when it does, I start praying. I can *feel* when something strange is coming.

And I felt it that night.

Somehow, though, I managed to fall asleep—sort of. And although I was dreaming, I knew that I was somewhere between complete wakefulness and sleep, and completely aware of my surroundings. And then, in the middle of a fairly ordinary dream, suddenly I was being attacked by demons.

For real.

I kept saying in my dream, "This is real. I need help." I started pleading the blood of Jesus—

--and I heard, "Open your eyes."

I did, out of a dead sleep. And to this day I have only spoken about what I saw just a few times. It scared the HELL out of me. I must have seen a dozen sets of glowing eyes. *Demons.*

I instantly came out of my sleep, pleading the blood of Jesus and asking for his protection. (Nothing will make you want some Jesus like a dozen demons.) I know this sounds crazy—look, it happened to me, and it made me *feel* crazy! But buckle up, because it gets worse.

Or maybe I should say, it gets better. Because what happened next made me realize that the experience I was having was very real. Because quite frankly, I am not smart enough or creative enough to be able to come up with something like this on my own.

I saw angels. Two of them! And—though I know this sounds very strange and incomprehensible, but maybe that's how you know it's real—they were both as big as buildings, but they fit inside my bedroom! I was able to see them from top to bottom and yet, at the same time, they were huge! And they were made of billions of multi-colored dots, colors and tones and shades I'd never seen before, swarming all over them.

Of course they had wings. But they weren't your normal, large, stately wings. These wings moved so fast, they made hummingbirds look frozen. One angel hovered over me and one stood near my husband. As soon as they appeared, the demons went away--and so did my fear. Which is not to say things went back to normal. Having an angel lay over the top of you is one of the most surreal experiences I have ever had. They were there for about twenty minutes, and the whole time I felt safe and free, coddled and protected. And I kept thinking, "This is really cool."

What else can you think at a time like that? I remember thinking, "There are demons in my bedroom! Help me,

Jesus!" and then there were giant angels in my bedroom. It seemed both completely bizarre and yet somehow normal — or, at least, real.

The angles disappeared, and all reverted to normal — and then I got scared. I turned on the light and my husband woke up and asked me what was wrong. I wasn't really sure how to explain it, but he knew by the look on my face that whatever had happened was real.

Still, to this day I am perplexed. I usually try and end each chapter or experience with some words of wisdom. Not this time. I can honestly say this thing left me speechless.

Chapter 11

Cindy the Homeless Lady

Growing up with a single parent raising three kids, watching my father work all the time, I had a great deal of respect for hard work and little to no compassion for lazy or unemployed people! I had started washing dishes at a restaurant when I was ten years old, working till late hours in the morning. When I was older I worked cleaning people's houses, babysitting, and doing all kinds of odd jobs in order to always have money in my pocket!

Maybe that's why, when I was thirty and encountered a homeless woman every day on my way to and from work, it bugged the hell out of me.

I had just bought a brand-new Volvo t5 (turbo) and *it was sweet!* I loved it. You see, I had not gotten a car until I was twenty-six years old — and I had worked my butt of to buy it. It was a Ford Festiva, but I was so thrilled to get it you would have thought I had acquired a Mercedes. It only had eleven thousand miles on it and I was officially its first owner. Getting that car was truly one of the greatest accomplishments of my twenties. I had tried and tried for years to get financed and every time I was told no.

The Volvo was my third car. Getting it had been a goal of mine and I was proud when I reached it. I planned to enjoy that car. I loved getting off work, opening my sunroof, and turning my music on.

But I couldn't enjoy it. Not fully, because there was that homeless lady on the street corner where I worked!

My job was selling manufactured homes. Our offices were in a large house. And every day, I would go to work, and that woman would be on that street corner, at 7:30 in the morning and all day — sometimes until 7:00 at night. She irritated me so badly! I couldn't stand her. All I wanted to do was drive to work and, after a full work day, drive home, and not have to see her. She looked as though she had not had a bath in ten years. I did everything possible to turn my head away or act like I couldn't see her.

Then the day came when I was so preoccupied with whatever was on my mind that I forgot to roll up my window--and there we were, face to face. She looked at me and smiled. And she had no front teeth. Also, I couldn't help but notice that her face was completely blistered from the sun. Her lips were cracked and bleeding.

I immediately got angry and said, "You know, if you had a job you wouldn't have to be out here every day, working twelve to fourteen hours begging. You could make more money than this *and* have a good life!" (I was really sure no one had ever told her that before.)

She put her head down in shame. I really didn't care. All I knew was that I had worked for everything I had. I had never asked or begged for anything. And, worse, the thought that a *women*, especially, would have to live this way, really bothered me.

She told me her name was Cindy. So for the next few months I would roll my window down and just say hello. Then one day I noticed that Cindy looked very different: Her eyes were blackened and she looked as though she had been beat up pretty badly. Plus, she was having a hard time sitting. I asked her what happened.

She said that her partner was a Vietnam Vet. He had night terrors and would sometimes beat her in his sleep. I was so disturbed I could barely work that day. I told her I was calling the police, but she asked me not to. The compassion she showed for him and his situation was amazing. I really had to take a step back and try and understand it.

So as time went on I started to pack her a lunch along with my own. Sometimes I would drop it off early in the morning, while she was still sleeping. Sometimes I would invite her up to eat on the porch of the house where our offices were, and we would eat together.

I learned a lot about Cindy. Her parents were deeply involved in politics--they were very busy and it doesn't sound like they had a lot of time for her. Still, that wasn't so unusual, and it certainly didn't explain her homelessness. I was really perplexed by her and her life. I truly could not understand where she took such a wrong a turn.

Plus, she was quite able to carry on a conversation; she had social skills, and manners, and grace. So, after about a year, I decided to stop trying to fix her. She was — at least she seemed--very happy and content doing what she was doing and living as she was living.

I gave her a tent and an umbrella. I also gave her clothes — *my husband's* old clothes, because she was well over six feet tall. But she never asked me for anything, ever.

Finally, one day I was looking at her through the sliding glass door of my office, and I closed my eyes and I prayed for her. I asked God, "Why? Why does Cindy have to be there?"

God replied, "So that you don't have to be."

I said, "What?"

God said, "Her life, her misery--it all has a purpose. Her purpose is to be seen by all the people driving by. They have their own ideas. Some are, *I would never do that.* Some are, *I feel like giving up.* Then they see her and she changes their mind. For some, it brings out their compassion. For a few, it changes their lives. She works for Me and keeps our society going by representing what you *don't* want to be."

I cried. In fact I cried a lot. I felt such remorse. I had always thought that the homeless somehow hurt us, that their purpose was nothing and their lives were nothing.

I look at everyone and everything differently now. I have an understanding of people and their purpose—or, rather, I should say I now try to figure out their purpose. Cindy was a good friend to me for many years. Then one summer she moved—supposedly to return in the fall, but I never saw her again. Now I drive by her spot every once in a while, and I think very fondly of her and how much she changed my life.

Thank you, Cindy, for teaching me compassion.

Chapter 12

$50

When I was 18 I was going to take the world by storm!

Like many 18-year-olds, I knew it all. The only thing I failed at was at a few life skills. And I needed a plan. So what! That's not much, right? I was sure it was all going to be fine.

After high school I moved out of the apartment I'd been living in and went to live with my sister. But I found out pretty quickly that she had taken the path of least resistance in life: Party hard, and then go to work. I could tell it was not the life for me. So I begged my parents for a bus ticket—and, if only to get rid of me, they gave me one. I used it to move to a big town (well, "big," anyway), where I thought there would be lots of opportunity.

It was a city of approximately 25,000 friendly people, all of whom, I was sure, were going to want to take care of me! I needed a job right away, so I applied at the local Hardees restaurant. Why not? It was right across the road from the room I had rented. I was going to work the night shift so I could get a day job as well. My rent was only $125, and I was making $3.25 an hour. I was going to be rich! True, I only worked 30 hours a week. But that was no problem, because my shift was from midnight to five in the morning. I would go home, sleep for a couple hours, and then walk to my next job (often in the snow). There I worked on commission all day, doing phone sales.

It sounded great — in theory. In fact, though, I was awful at it. I was tired. Along with being tired, I was really hungry. I mean REALLY hungry. One day I got the bright idea that I could eat chicken gizzards and crackers. They were both cheap and I liked them. So I plunged into The Chicken Gizzard Diet. I loved 'em!

I was about a month into my enriched diet when some hot grease I was cooking with hit the paper towels, which fell over and set a curtain on fire. Thank God I was quick to act--and my old boyfriend and his father were at my front door and helped me out. The result was that I was no longer allowed to fry anything on my small, apartment-sized cooktop. So much for the Chicken Gizzard Diet.

Besides not having much to eat, I faced the necessity of washing my clothes as well. It was expensive to go to the Laundromat and I just couldn't afford it. One day, though, I was lying in bed and hit upon a brilliant plan: I would just start going home on the weekends to eat and do my laundry. I could catch a ride with the mailman from my hometown, who went back and forth almost every day.

And that's what I did, confident I had the best plan ever. And it worked perfectly--until I walked into my house, my stepmother took one look at me, and said, "Don't plan on coming home with your laundry every weekend."

I was crushed. I sat downstairs all weekend long. I cried a lot and I said to God, "I need a break! I am so hungry, Lord. I need food. Please help me."

It just so happened that, before my parents had bought the house, it had been the home of a woman in her late 90's. She had kept the place immaculate. She left behind a lot of old bottles and a bookshelf full of books. Now I heard God say, "Stand up and go to the bookcase." I thought I was hearing things. I heard it again and again. I kept looking around to see if someone was talking to me, because it sounded just like God—or, at least, someone--was right beside me. I finally got up and walked over to the bookcase and opened it.

The voice said, "Now pull out a book." I felt really foolish by now, but why not? I said, "Okay, okay..." I pulled a book out.

The voice said, "Now open it." I did. And inside the book was a crisp $50 bill. I started literally jumping for joy. I couldn't believe it. But then I got scared. I thought, *What if this money is my parents'?* So I asked them both if they had any books in the bookcase. They both said, not only did they have no books in the book case, neither of them had ever even opened it.

That's when I knew that money was for me. I took it and bought a hamburger. I don't know if it was the best burger I'd ever eaten, but at that moment I was fuller than I had been in months. I took the rest of the money home and was very careful with it. In fact the only splurge I used it for was to buy a newspaper so that I could look for a better job. And I got one. I saw an ad for an agency hiring nannies. I signed up and a few weeks later I moved to Boston. It was a long time before I was hungry again.

God is good. He takes care of us when we can't. Any time I'm confronted with the impossible, when I'm afraid, when I can't figure something out, I recall that day when God knew I needed Him and he saved me. And over my lifetime I have tried to keep a lucky $50 on me, so that when God tells me to bless someone with it, I do!

Chapter 13

My Mother

I have really tried to write these chapters in the order of the happiness these events have brought me. But this one is really difficult.

My mother died when I was the ripe old age of four. I am not really sure what my life would have been like with her, but I can tell you how hard it has been without her. I don't know if you ever really heal from losing a mother--I think it's something that aches in your heart forever. When you're a child, it seems that, no matter what your friends have or don't have--a bike, a Barbie, whatever—*everybody* has a Mom. You really feel that on Mothers Day, which was a day of complete awkwardness for me until I had my own children. And, if you're a girl, you feel it on every occasion at which only a mother's advice will help: your first period, a first kiss, a first love…not to mention the never-ending need of instruction in how to cook and, of course, how to be a mother.

My father had gotten remarried to a woman who…well, let's say she really didn't have a great appreciation for me. I have a very unusual spirit, and a personality you either love to love or love to hate. I could deal with that among my peers. But living with someone who loved to hate you—an *adult*, who never tired of it--was more than a teenage child should have to bear. So my home life was hell. My father drank a lot and was very physically abusive. The turmoil was constant, day in and day out, and I was a nervous wreck.

I tried to babysit and do volunteer work, or take any odd jobs that came along—anything, just to get out of the house. And when I did that, and was able to see how other families lived, I yearned to live like they did. My Girl Scout leader had (or so I thought) the perfect life. Her home was beautiful. Her cookies were perfect. Her daughter had a pink and white room. Her Christmas tree was amazing, I can't tell you the mental notes I used to make of her life and her home.

But these fantasies and wishes came at a price: The more time I spent at other places, the more depressed I got. You'd think that creating a family would be a simple and natural thing. But to me it felt like the hardest thing in the world to achieve.

I was sixteen years old and getting more and more depressed. I felt like my life was just spinning out of control. My Father was drinking more and more, and he was not getting along with his wife. I had broken up with my cheating boyfriend. It seemed to me that life really didn't have that much to offer.

One night I had come home from babysitting to a storm of crazy, with lots of arguing and fighting. I went downstairs to my bedroom in "the dungeon." And I just wept. I was sick of living like this and, really, was just sick of living, period. I lay my head down, closed my eyes, and asked God to take me...I was tired and worn out. I wanted to go and be with my Mother. I knew she would be happy to see me…

All of a sudden I was standing there *with my mother.* It was amazing. It was unreal. We were in a café, talking and laughing. I couldn't believe it. She was absolutely the most beautiful person in the whole world. Even her dress was amazing, a fantastic green.

I said, "Mom! Does Dad know you're here?"

She smiled and said, "No."

I said, "He would be so happy to see you!"

We talked about how much I missed her and how badly I needed her and how much I hated my life without her. And she told me that it was okay — that she missed me, too, and that I could go with her! I felt such an extraordinary amount of love in those few minutes, I honestly can't explain it.

I said, "Okay, I'll go. But first let's go see Dad and say goodbye."

She told me we could do that, but he wouldn't be able to see us. Still, we went, and I was so happy to have us all together. She also gave me a peek at how Dad felt on the inside--and it was very sad. Even on my worst day I never felt like he did. I actually felt bad for him and for his life. It occurred to me that I had my whole life ahead of me, but he didn't. This was his life, and it would most likely be like this forever.

Meanwhile, I knew that, no matter what, my life would be nothing like his.

And suddenly I experienced a sense of peace that I hadn't had in a really long time. The longing to die left me. I wanted to live. I turned to tell my mother that--and she was gone. It was as though she knew she had accomplished what she had come to do.

From that day on, I had a change of heart about many things and many people. I realized that holding on to anger was a really sad approach to life, and that, like a disease, it can be extremely contagious.

Now I look at it like this: I get a flu shot of love every morning from God. He protects me. He gives me the opportunity to spread some other kind of "infectious" thing--the germ of faith. It's the opposite of a disease; it's a blessing. Once you find the peace of God, everything else in life is calm, placid, and still.

Chapter 14

Paul

Paul was an amazing human being. In the short time he was alive he did more than most people do who live to be a hundred. At only twenty-seven years old he spoke seven languages, had worked for the CIA, and had a plethora of awards and accolades bestowed upon him. He played the piano like a concert pianist. The thing I loved about him the most was his love for God. He was a devout Catholic and donated his time to the Newman center.

But Paul had had a terrible, life-changing accident that had left him with *grand mal* seizures. He had accidentally fallen off a third-floor stairwell and was in a coma for about four months. They didn't think he would make it. Amazingly, he did, but his life would never be the same. He would never be able to drive a car, or even ride a bicycle. He'd never be able to hold a baby. He had had so much talent, and it had been taken away.

I was in property management and Paul was one of our tenants. We immediately became good friends. I spent all my spare time with him. He used to sing and play the guitar for my daughter, Lauren. He became a very special friend to us.

Then one day his life took a turn for the worse, if you can believe that. Paul was in a car accident. It triggered a *grand mal* seizure, during which he ended up really hurting himself. His leg was badly injured and he was hospitalized for months. During his hospitalization Paul met a pretty nurse. They were soon married.

I was not invited to the wedding.

Paul's new wife and his pretty friend didn't see eye to eye, so the friend—me--got the boot. I tried to act like I wasn't hurt, but in fact I was devastated. I really liked having him in my life. Paul and his wife moved out of our building and started their lives together. Then, about three weeks later (it might have been longer but for some reason I don't think so), some friends of his came into my office, where Paul had left some crutches for them to pick up.

I was dying to ask about the wedding, about Paul and his new wife, about their life together. The friends and I talked for a few minutes and I finally had the courage to ask, "So, how is the happy couple?"

Their faces turned white. "Didn't you hear? Paul died."

They think that his medication was off and he got depressed and shot himself. I could barely breathe. I thought I was hearing something that couldn't possibly be true. I couldn't even put words together. I will never forget the shock.

I went home and I prayed and cried and prayed and cried. I asked God, first, "Why?" And second, over and over, I prayed, "Please, Lord, I need to know he is not in pain." I begged God to tell me.

I missed the next few days of work. I spent them on the floor, right by my front door where I had dropped the second I had walked into my apartment. I didn't eat. I didn't move. I cried until the blood vessels in my eyes broke. It was one of the most sorrowful times of my life.

On the third day I went to see Paul's gravestone. He had been buried in a very special place--at a monastery, which I thought that would be so fitting for him. I came home from the gravesite and I felt like I was getting worse. I felt like I would never smile again. I went to bed that night and prayed and asked God to please explain to me what and why.

The next part of this is unbelievable. I have never experienced anything like it before or since.

I went to sleep for the first time in three days. And I started dreaming. But suddenly, in my dream, I felt like I was awake and sitting up. I could see myself (and my daughter). And then, suddenly, I was transported to a place

I had never been. The only way I can explain to you what it was like is to say: There are no words to explain what it was like. I experienced an incredible calm and indescribable beauty, and a feeling of love that I had surely never felt in this life. The colors, the sense of space, the sensation of amazement were truly unreal. I asked where I was, and I heard "Heaven." It felt like I was there for a lifetime.

I remember everything and yet, somehow, I remember nothing. The things I know for sure are, that I came away knowing very clearly, is that everything happens for a reason—even really bad things. I also came away with the understanding—at least I think I understand it—is that your mind is your soul.

That really freaked me out. Because I know for a fact that the self I present to the world is better than the mind I live with inside my head. That may be true about a lot of people, but it's sure true about me. So if your mind is your soul, then I came back from that experience knowing that I needed to work on improving my mind. And that-- controlling my mind--is not easy. So the prospect of having to do that scared me.

Then I heard, "You need to go back," and found myself begging to stay. Whoever or whatever was talking to me reminded me that I had a daughter who needed me—and, of course, that's all it took. I remember entering my body and sitting straight up, almost gasping for air, completely freaked out. I kept saying over and over, "My mind is my soul? My mind is my soul?" I looked at the edge of my bed. It was a waterbed, and there was a big indentation there even though no one was sitting there. And then, suddenly, it was gone, and the bed started to slosh around.

Everything about that night is completely unexplainable. I tried to account for it by telling myself, Well, babe, it's because of lack of food and sleep. But I have to tell you, nothing in my life--my experiences, my sadness over Paul, anything I'd ever done or thought--could have ever given me the feelings, the emotions, the ideas, the thoughts, the dreams, or *whatever* that I had that night. I found out that Paul was well, and I woke up whole. I never cried again over losing him.

Since then I have I tried to live my mental life differently. I mean I've tried to keep my mind purer. Paul, I think, was an angel in my life, a blessing. His life was tragically beautiful.

Amazing was your life, Paul, and so was your friendship. I will miss you all my days, but I am content to know that all things happen for a reason. Love you.

Chapter 15

The Edging

Reader, I'm not sure you'll appreciate this chapter as much as the others, but I really need to write it. Why? For many reasons--but one in particular stands out: how closely God listens to us. Even when we are not praying, but just *talking* to Him, the way we'd talk to a friend (or, should I say, a best friend), He listens. He is a true partner in my life, a confidante.

Steve and I were having major money troubles. Like most young couples, we were trying to raise a family on a budget. We had two children at the time, and had bought our first home. (We still live in it!) Our baby had just been born the night before we closed on the house. We weren't aware of all the extra expenses that came with having a new home--and we had also forgotten about the expenses of having a new baby. (This wasn't our fault. Our other child was already nine years old.)

So we were overwhelmed, to say the least. Still, we learned to manage without much — those were the bean and rice years--and we were happy.

I am a gardener and I love my backyard. I would sometimes go out there and stare, trying to imagine what the yard would look when it was done and complete. (Although, as any gardeners reading this know, it's *never* done or complete.) I knew that, on our budget, it would be a really long time before it would even come close to being done. But as an optimist I would just let my mind go and dream.

My husband's family is from Germany — and I mean *off the boat* from Germany. One of the things I love, if not the best thing that I love, about my husband is, his love for his family and of his nationality. The whole family celebrates being German. Christmas Eve is goulash and Christmas Day is schnitzel. They speak German when they are all together, so when my kids visit with them it's an international experience. I love giving my kids a multicultural life--I think it makes their lives less one-dimensional and makes them open to the differences in others.

Now, about every year or so my husband and his brothers are sent back to Germany by their parents. His Grandfather still lives there — or, rather, he did at the time this story happened. (He has since passed.) The boys were very close to their Grandfather, who they called "Opa." Although his parents always paid for the trip (Note to them: Thank you thank you thank you!!!!), there were always other expenses that went along with him being gone. There were expenses here and in Germany and we just didn't have two pennies to rub together.

So Steve was gone and we were broke. I remember thinking, *Lord, please just make these next ten days go fast and smooth.* I had a lot of time by myself to think and look in the backyard and talk to God about how I would like to fix it up.

I remember standing and looking outside from the window one morning and saying--not praying—*Lord, I would really like some edging to go all the way around the yard. Concrete would be nice.*

Do you know what I mean by edging? It's a series of lengths of concrete or wood, about four to six inches high, that you lay along the border of a lawn or a garden. It's like a decorative trim to finish off a border. It comes in different shapes, like rocks or bricks, but also in lengths with a scalloped top.

Anyway, that's what I talked to the Lord about—edging. Then I walked away and didn't think about it again. That was Monday. The rest of the week was great. The kids and I were fine; all was content even though Steve was gone. He was having fun and so were we.

I was taking Sabina to school that Friday morning and I saw a yard sale sign. So I started to turn in the direction of the sale. But I yelled at myself, *Wait a minute! You have no money!* I knew what was in my purse, and when I looked in my ashtray I only had one nickel! *What are you doing??*

So I straightened the car out and kept taking my daughter to school. On the way back, I wasn't even thinking of anything--I was just driving — when, all of the sudden, I found myself turning where the yard sale sign was. *What are you doing Brittany???*

Oh my, I started saying to myself. *You don't have any money.* But, strangely, I didn't stop. Yes, I was yelling at myself but I didn't stop. To this day don't I understand it.

I turned into this subdivision, still driving and still yelling. If you had seen me you would have thought I was crazy. Finally I see the last YARD SALE sign, and I see the house, and what else do I see? STACKS AND STACKS OF CEMENT EDGING WITH A BIG SIGN THAT SAYS *FREE!!*

All I have to say is, I could barely contain myself. God immediately reminded me of my conversation with Him, and I could see Him smile. As a matter of fact, I could *feel* Him smile.

It was enough for my entire yard. I have it to this day!!

I encourage you to treat the Lord as your friend. Talk to Him. Ask Him to guide you in all things. I speak to the Lord as though I have Him over for dinner, or we're drinking lemonade together. He is my friend; I actually talk to Him more than I pray. I am not always right and proper in what I say. But what I figured out is, He has an ear, and He wants you to go to Him about everything. I talk to him about decorating, about what's for dinner…EVERYTHING!!

Try it, and see the change in your life!!!

Chapter 16

Blue Laws

By the time I was in the seventh grade I was crazy in love with a boy who I had been dreaming about forever—meaning, since fourth grade.

I prayed every night, from the seventh grade on, that I would marry him. And, when I was twenty years old, I did! I was so excited; I couldn't believe my dreams had come true. He was tall and handsome and a hard worker. We had dated on and off while we were in school. The "off" came mostly because he would find someone else to be "on" with, but I held on. I was nuts about him and would have sold my soul to marry him. Thirty-three years ago, on May 5th I married him.

We'll call him my first husband. Because, that's right: we're divorced.

With marriage came a lot of responsibility and a need for understanding—which were both talents I apparently didn't have. As you know by now, I had grown up in a very dysfunctional household. I had no mother in the home.

And, although I had grandparents and aunts and uncles who were very proper, who never swore or drank too much, who went to church and had perfect homes and were well dressed at all times — the fact was I had none of that in my own home as I was growing up.

Of course, I was able to witness what I *thought* perfection looked like. I logged more hours of *Leave it to Beaver* and other TV shows than anyone I knew. From them I learned that wives had dinner on the table--and that it was good. Wives kept a clean house that was well-decorated. Wives looked good at all times. That was all I knew about being a wife, but it seemed to be enough, and it was what I wanted to achieve.

I have since learned that what I saw on TV and what was real were two completely different things. Somehow, television shows failed to inform me about what to do if your husband doesn't come home at night. Or what to do when strange women start calling the house. Or what to do about the lipstick-stained cigarettes that turn up in the car when your husband doesn't smoke. None of that appeared on episodes of *Leave it to Beaver*.

Also my reaction--I'm a wild-haired Italian girl whose temper could peel paint--wasn't covered.

It gradually dawned on both of us that this wasn't going to work. I really don't know what happened, other than to suggest that my ideals didn't match up with reality. I want to say that he cheated first, and that's what caused it all to fall apart. But I don't think that's what happened. Rather, I think that we as a couple were very immature. We didn't know how to *be* married. Whereas we're both married to other people now, and both marriages have lasted. My ex has had a wife for twenty-plus years and I've been with my husband for twenty three-plus years. But I think each of us needed to fail at that first marriage in order to learn what we each had to learn.

I took the divorce very hard. (He didn't.) It was life-changing for me; it set me on a journey of wellness and understanding, because I really wanted to know that that first marriage was not a mistake. Bear in mind that, while growing up in that dysfunctional hell of a household, I was very careful *not* to make mistakes. I calculated every step I made. So when the divorce happened it was really hard on me. We had had a child together and I also (to throw something else into the mix) had gotten Pica with the pregnancy and we had, at least at first, survived that.[1]

---

1   Pica is associated with children who eat dirt, who are born with learning deficiencies. In rare occurrences, it is manifested by pregnant women. My mother actually had it. It took me two pregnancies to find out what it was--and it almost cost me my second husband as well. Because when I had it, it made me crazy, crazier than a cat in a bag. First, you think that you are completely normal. You are not. You eat ice or worse. You feel normal and you think you are acting normal. You are not. You believe how you are feeling is real. It is not. So there is no rational with the irrational. After about a year, it goes away. This also put great stress on my first marriage—although I would like to say in a side note that my current husband has gone through three pregnancies with me and never left my side. He has great character.

As our marriage fell apart I really couldn't believe that I had made a mistake. After all, I had prayed about getting married to him since I was in the seventh grade! I was sure that God had answered my prayers when I married him.

Now I prayed and asked God, *Lord, if this marriage is Your will, then I need you to supernaturally stop this divorce.* (Mind you, David, my husband, was already living with the other woman). Although saving the marriage, to me, was not the point. The point was, *I wanted to know that I had not made a mistake with my life's decision.*

I went down to the courthouse and found out that if you petitioned for it, you could force your spouse to get marriage counseling at least one time. I thought, Well, once is better than nothing.

So what I did was, I fasted. And prayed. And asked God, *Lord, if this is what you wanted for my life, then stop this divorce. Even if, in the end, I get divorced, I want to know that I did not go outside of Your will.*

We went to the counselor, and David told him, over and over, what a terrible wife and person I was. And I thought, *This is weird. The man keeps smiling and almost giggling at us. Strange reaction from a counselor.* I thought, *This guy is getting a kick out of my pain.*

My husband looked at me like he hated me and wanted nothing to do with me. It was a good thing I had been fasting for a few days, because I think that I would have thrown up then and there. I kept saying in my head, *God, this isn't going the way I wanted. Lord, this is really going in the wrong direction.* I wanted to give up. I kept thinking about what a fool I'd made of myself. I wanted the whole thing over with.

All of a sudden, the counselor stood up and said, "Man, you're just mad at her and trying to punish her. You're going to regret this decision the rest of your life. Decisions made in anger aren't ever right ones."

He then went on to say, "Our state has something called a blue law. It's a law that's been on the books but that no one ever uses. It's a law that, if a counselor thinks your marriage can be saved and you're are getting a divorce for the wrong reasons, he can petition the court and stop the divorce. And that is what I am planning on doing."

This law had never been enforced before. This was the first time. And I thought I was going to pass out. God had answered my prayers! I hadn't made a mistake. I had married who God had intended. Now, if the divorce happened, it would be due to my husband's will—not mine, and not God's.

My husband missed the next counseling appointment. His attendance had been a direct order from the judge, and he had to answer for that. And we ended up getting divorced.

God blessed me over and over after that. He put people into my life to care for me, and He opened doors that I could never have thought of going through. I changed my life, not only out of my sheer will, but out of His will.

So look: life will throw you some curveballs--sometimes a lot of them. You will never have control over someone else's decisions even if they affect you. You have to ask God to protect you, to lead you through every situation. Ask Him to work His will. (You'll still be plenty busy working your own, and there will be hard work attached to it.) I know this sounds crazy, but I firmly believe that 100% of the time you will triumph. In the end you will get everything you need.

Chapter 17

Happy 21st Birthday, Bunny

Giving birth to my first child, Lauren, was the most amazing, beautiful, and scary thing that I have ever done.

Bear in mind that, like most first-time mothers, I had zero idea of what I was doing. I asked a nurse if I had to burp my baby if she was nursed (she said no) that was not right. And while becoming a mom meant dealing with a huge learning curve, with lots of hits and misses, it went really fast and I enjoyed every minute of it.

Until my daughter was nine, it was just the two of us, so we had some pretty lean times--but nothing God didn't get us through. I swear I ate peanut butter and jelly sandwiches every day, for four years. (I seemed to get sick every time I ate one, too. Finally, years later, I learned I was allergic to peanuts.)

I always gave her a birthday party, but I particularly dreamed of the big ones: 1,13, 16 and, of course, her 21st. I tried to do something special for every one of them, but for those particular ones I really wanted to celebrate her life--and I did. We had big, big parties for all of them!

Well, almost all.

It was going to be her 21st and I was so excited. I had just given birth to my fourth child at the end of March. Lauren's birthday was in August, so although I was a wee bit tired, I knew I had some time to prepare the huge party I had planned for her. I wanted to order a cake—huge; two stories tall--from the nicest bakery in town. I was going to take our entire family—all the uncles, aunts, and cousins--to this fabulous, over-the-top Italian restaurant. I was going to order every hors d'oeuvre on the menu. Oh, and the gift—well, that, too, would be over the top. This was going to be a no-expense-spared event. She was going to know, and believe, that we were celebrating her and her life.

Then a phone call came.

The job that I had had for the past eight years, that I loved and had made more money at than all my other jobs put together, the job that would pay for Lauren's party…was over. The company had closed their doors overnight.

I canceled everything. I knew in my gut not to spend a dime. Not only me--I knew that hard times for the US were around the corner. And I was right! (I should have opened a psychic hotline.) Times were real tough.

I remember sitting in the chair, wondering what we were going to do about my angel's birthday. My last check was all gone. I had paid $12,000 in advertising costs up front, and now the company that was supposed to reimburse me for it no longer existed.

Worse, we had to pay for Lauren's college in one week, and it was too late to get loans. Not to mention the $96,000 worth of contracts that I had personally signed for. We were beside ourselves.

I sat down one day and looked up and asked God to please, please bless my daughter with a gift. A wonderful gift that would be her heart's desire. A gift that I would know could only come from you God and you alone. I looked out the window and prayed. It was a very humble prayer.

The phone rang. It was Lauren. I told her that I had just prayed for a miracle for her birthday, and to buckle up, because it would be big.

Now, Lauren was just heading to her job. She worked at Mac Cosmetics and she was an amazing makeup artist. She really enjoyed what she did, and it helped her get through school. She always said, "Mom, I wish I could have a whole makeup brush set, so I could do freelance makeup." Well, that kind of thing would run thousands of dollars. So for her birthday I thought that I would just start out by getting her the portable makeup chair. And then, each holiday and birthday, I could get her a few brushes until she had everything she needed. I prayed and prayed every morning, looking out the window asking God for her miracle.

Well.

On the fourth morning, while I was getting ready to pray, my phone rang. And she was screaming and screaming, "Mom! Mom! I can't believe this! Mother, I was helping Austin..." (He was the cute boyfriend at the time.) "...move, and we were putting things away. And there was an extra box. I asked him whose it was it was. It was black and all wrapped up. He said, 'That must be my roommate's.'" So Lauren took it to his room, he said, "It's not mine." They all looked at each other and no one knew whose bag it was. So Lauren sat down and opened it.

Not only was it *a complete set of makeup brushes,* but it also had all the specialty brushes, *and* special nail brushes! There were over 100 brushes in this set! Along with an apron to hold them all. IT WAS A COMPLETE PROFESSIONAL MAKEUP ARTIST KIT.

We were also able to take Lauren to dinner. It wasn't as big a spread as I'd planned, but we went with the aunts and sister to the same place I wanted to take her. She said it was the best birthday she had ever had.

God is good. He takes care of us. All we have to do is ask with an open heart and expect an answer.

Chapter 18

Mary

This is probably the most embarrassing chapter, because it reveals some very poor behavior on my part.

I was thirty years old and had been married about a year. I loved my home and my neighborhood when I moved in. For a tract house, ours was a beautiful home, and I loved the neighborhood. The streets were wide and the front yards were beautiful. It was a fairytale life--

--until one morning I woke up and it was over. I walked outside and saw a new neighbor. As I was about to say hello, she started running with her broom and chasing her child, yelling, "You little @#$%##^! I'm going to beat your #^$(%($!"

I was in shock. The image of my perfect neighborhood was in ruins, destroyed by a pink-slipper-wearing, broom-wielding, pajama-clad crazy woman chasing her kid. I went into the house and screamed, "Steven! Put the house up for sale! You will not *believe* what moved in down the block."

Things spiraled down from there. This woman had cars--lots of them, parked all over the front yard. They were "fixer-uppers," which is a polite way of saying, wrecks. There was one that remained on jacks for four years. It was appalling! I hated those people. I hated them for ruining my perfect block! And I swore that I would never, ever have anything to do with them!

Years and years go by. I walk or drive by their house and I get more and more bitter every time I see that car still up on its jacks, or the plethora of cars in front of their home, all probably leaking oil. I can't explain how mad I am. I have decided that I want my new house NOW, and I want it FAST. By then I have a great job and was making good money. And so was my husband. And yet, I can't find land to build my new house on! It doesn't seem to be working out for me and I can't understand why. Every piece of land I look at, has something wrong with it. Or has problems. Meanwhile, every one of our friends and family have all gotten their new homes--except for me! Why?

I woke up one morning depressed and asked God, *Why do I not have my house? I do everything I am supposed to. So why, Lord, why?*

I hear, in a very loud and stern voice, "BECAUSE YOU HAVE NOT APPRECIATED THE ONE I HAVE GIVEN YOU."

What?! That is ridiculous! I have *too*! Look at this house! It's beautiful.

The Lord said, in maybe not so loud and stern a voice, "Not only have you not appreciated your house, but you aren't even nice to your neighbors. Be nice and appreciate your home, and then things in your life will change."

I said, *I don't agree with You, Lord.* (I know you think that by now I would listen to and agree with everything God said to me. But I felt that He couldn't tell me my opinions about things.) *I do appreciate my home!! So, no changes!!*

A year goes by—a year during which I have made good on my promise: No changes! Now I am six months pregnant with my fourth child, and a bit cranky. I am in no mood for any foolishness. I go to check my mail and what do I see? Mary's car, still up on jacks. As usual.

And I just reached my limit. Because ugh! *How many years do I have to look at this!* All I can think is, her husband must be lazy. And then what do I see? It's Mary! Outside!

"Mary!" I roar. "When are you going to take that eyesore of a car down off those jacks?"

Mary looks at me very nicely and says, "We can't afford the new tires the car needs."

What? It never occurred to me that that would be the reason! All of a sudden I hear the Lord's voice again, saying, "Be nice to your neighbors."

So I say, "Well, Mary, I do finance. Come over later and I'll figure it out for you."

She and her husband came over later that evening. I sat down with them and figured everything out. I refinanced their home, paid off a bunch of their bills, and got them off on a new start. And while I was doing their loan, I learned some things about Mary:

First, she and her husband were very cute together. While they were with me he had his arm around her the whole time, or was holding her hand. They had been together since she was sixteen. They had been married a long time. She was a very devoted mother and—even with the broom and the screaming—loved her children a lot. She also volunteered her time and home to F.A.I.R. (an organization that fosters animals). She had 19 pets in her home at one time, on average. She also took really good care of her mother-in-law and an elderly neighbor.

There was a part of me that felt bad about what I had thought of Mary all these years. Could I have been wrong, and God right? Hmm! Well, I'm still in the discovery phase of my idiocy.

Then there was my home--you know, the one I ignored God's word about because I supposedly took such good care of it. We had decided to put hardwood floors in upstairs. The carpet was 13 years old and very worn. So, to do that, of course, we had to empty the upstairs. I worked until three in the morning, getting everything done. I woke up the next day and went upstairs—

--and was shocked. I mean amazed. That home that I took such good care of? It looked like a gang of vagabonds lived there. The walls were a mess! How long had it been since I painted them? The doors were horrible! I was astounded.

I was also very embarrassed. And once again I heard the Lord's voice: "APPRECIATE YOUR HOME."

I couldn't believe what I had done. I truly had *not* appreciated my home. I just wanted the next new thing instead of being grateful for what I had. So I painted the whole upstairs and remodeled the house.

As for Mary, I started making soup for her and her family. And then one day, my trusty dog, Mozart, died after eleven years of the happiest time. Mary came to me and held me like a baby. She cried with me and was a real friend. I apologized that day, and told her how much I hadn't liked her. I asked for her forgiveness. I explained to her that I was a fool and had missed out on what a good person and neighbor she had been.

Now I count Mary and her family as not only friends, but as *good* friends. I thank God for that lesson and am very grateful. Guess what, Lord--You were right!! Thank you, Lord, for Mary!

Chapter 19

God Sold My Car

This really is just plain and simple, but it blew my mind!

I purchased a new car and needed to sell my old one. I had never really sold a car before. I wasn't sure what the liabilities were, or what I had to do--so the car just sat there, month after month. I would go outside sometimes and start it up, and make sure the windows stayed clean, but other than that, it just sat there. I thought and thought about it. I even thought maybe I'd give it away. I really needed the money but I just didn't know what I was doing.

So I was sitting in my rocking chair one day, thinking about the car, and I thought, "I know this is ridiculous, but I'm going to ask God to either sell my car or show me what to do with it." So I prayed: *Lord, I do not know how to sell a car. I have no idea what I'm doing. So if you would like me to give my car away, show me to whom. But if not, could you please bring me a buyer?*

I was happy with my prayer and thought, "I wonder when I'll get my answer..." I settled back to watch my afternoon movie on the Hallmark Channel. And about forty minutes later a man came and knocked on my door, and asked me if I would like to sell my car!

I thought it was a joke. In fact I walked outside and looked around, to see—somehow; I didn't know how--if it *was* a joke. But it was just him, with a puzzled look on his face. I felt like someone had just hit me in the head with a brick. I was in such shock! I asked him, "Did someone tell you the car was for sale?"

"No," he replied.

I asked him, "Then why did you stop?"

He said, "Well, I liked it, and wondered if you wanted to sell it. I was driving through the neighborhood on a service call, and I saw this SUV, and thought I'd stop and ask. I've wanted one for a while."

So we arranged for him to come back the next night with his wife, and test drive it. I was out that next evening, and my husband called and said that a guy and his wife had given the car a test drive, and then handed over $7,000 and bought the car.

So when I tell you "God sold my car," it means *He sold my car*. That was the fastest and craziest answered prayer ever. It showed me supernaturally how quickly God acts when you let go. I remember praying something like, *I have no need to control this*. I had let go because I had no idea what to do. I learned a lot about letting go of control that day, and about how truly simple prayers can be.

I also learned—again--that we serve a literal God. Nothing is too big or too small for Him—including selling a car for you. Your problems are His. Treat him like your best friend. Talk to him about decorating. Or nail polish. Or your dreams.

Chapter 20

Thank You, God, for My Grandpa

There are special people and there are *special people*.

My grandfather had the greatest impact on my life. He was self-educated, self-motivated, and made his own world in a town of—well, as of 2017, it was a town with a population of 55.

He had a museum in his backyard. He was notorious all over the state for owning a steam engine. And no one could miss him with his infamous red and white polka-dotted hat!

My grandfather was amazing. He would recite poetry and Bible verses to me, and could explain things in a way unlike anyone else. He was the only person whose every word I believed every time. He never cared what people thought. I never heard him gossip or swear. He had a great admiration and respect for God that made a great impression upon me.

So I was devastated when I received a phone call (that I was somehow expecting) that he had been killed in a car accident. "Expecting"?

Yes. The week before, I was at a resort in Medora, N.D. I had been working there all summer long, drinking and partying like a rockstar. On a Thursday night, two weeks before I was to go home and start my senior year of high school, I woke up from a disturbing dream:

I had walked into a lighthouse. (I'm not sure why, because I had never seen one before.) The lighthouse almost seemed to be glowing, as though drawing me near. I went in, where I was met by an angel, who walked me slowly up some stairs until I reached the very top. I entered a room in which someone lay on a surface, under a sheet. I was scared to approach, but the angel guided me. He pulled the sheet back and showed me my grandfather. I screamed and woke up.

I knew then that I had to go home. I went to the office the next morning and told them that my grandfather had died. I was under contract and had to be released. I left that Friday morning without even saying goodbye to my boyfriend; I couldn't wait to get home. I arrived there without even having told my parents I was coming. All was well at home. I thought, *Dang! I could have stayed and had fun for one more week. Oh well!*

Then, a week to the day--when I *should* have been on my way home--the phone rang. It was my grandmother's neighbor. She told me that my grandfather had been killed earlier that day in a car accident. He had been driving, and apparently had looked into the sun and didn't see a car coming. It hit him directly on the driver's side. He was killed instantly.

God knew that I could not handle that news away from home. I believe God allowed that dream to motivate me to go home, so I'd be there when this tragedy took place. It was one of the few times in my life I was brought to my knees in sorrow.

But, as a matter of fact, the other time also involved my grandfather in a dream.

I was married to my first husband. We had a child (Lauren, whom you've already read about). She was just a baby. I thought life—especially considering my past--was perfect. But then I had that dream…

In the dream I was with my very good-looking, almost movie star-handsome grandfather. He wore a Fedora hat, slightly tilted, and his beige trench coat. We were in a cemetery. I yelled, "Grandpa!" He gave me a great big hug and asked me to walk with him. He started to explain that I was going to go through a very hard time soon--I was going to be getting a divorce. I was going to take it very hard. But he wanted me to know that I would make it through, that he loved me and was always with me. I was going to feel like I wanted to die, but he told me to resist that feeling, that my life would be great. It would be hard but I would be okay. He told me things in a way that only he could. And I believed him.

I woke up in the morning and looked at my husband and asked him if we were getting a divorce that somehow I didn't know about. Well, the look on his face said it all! It was the beginning of the end. I found out within a few days that he had fallen for another.

Shortly after that he filed for divorce — and, true to my grandfather's words, I wanted to die! I stopped eating and shrunk down to 97 pounds. I became a whole new kind of crazy. It took time, a lot of Jesus, and faith in the knowledge that this, too, would pass to get me through it.

Now, also true to my grandfather's word, life is great! I have four kids and an amazing husband of almost 23 years! God knew what I needed, and gave it to me when I needed it. I am so much better for having gone through that divorce--a better person, more aware, more feeling, and more forgiving. It's what I needed to set my life on the right track. I thank God for His willingness to allow me to suffer, and for the growth that I experienced because of it.

Chapter 21

Coming off the Mountain

Now this one is really strange.

It all started with my children wanting to see the Grand Canyon. We were just coming back from a trip to the Midwest—me, and a car full of kids and luggage, with movies being played over and over. We had reached the Grand Canyon right before the park was going to close. But we had driven so far out of the way that we decided to go ahead and we went in anyway.

I have to say I was a bit disappointed. After all, I had grown up around the Black Hills of South Dakota, and thought that they were prettier. And we had driven such a long way! So we stayed for about fifteen minutes, until I started to get bored. I told the kids we needed to leave. Besides, it was going to get dark soon, and I have a hard time driving in the dark. So we packed back up to the car and away we went.

We had a five-hour drive ahead of us and it was getting dark fast. I should by no means ever drive at night without my glasses, but where they were, I had no idea. I just know that I had my children and my niece in the car, and I felt like it was a very dangerous situation. I asked the kids to help me see and keep an eye out, but as time passed I grew more and more afraid.

I decided I needed some Holy Ghost assistance, because I was about to have a meltdown in front of all those kids. It was pitch black out and there were no other cars in sight. We were on a curvy, winding road, coming down a mountain, and all I could think of was the movie *The Other Side of the Mountain*, in which a girl has a horrible accident.

I started to pray and ask God to help me. I prayed and prayed, but still I thought I was going to pepper my windshield with vomit, I was so wound up. My niece was sitting beside me in the front, listening to my prayers as they got louder and louder. I could tell my anxiety was getting to her and the other kids. She kept saying, "Auntie, it's going to be fine." But we kept going around and around that mountain and it felt like it was taking forever.

All of a sudden I couldn't take it anymore. Ahead and below us I could see city lights. It looked like they were really far away, but also like they were straight down. The road kept winding and winding and all I could think was that we were going to go over the edge and plunge straight down.

I screamed, "GOD, I NEED OFF THIS MOUNTAIN RIGHT NOW! IN THE NAME OF JESUS!"

All of a sudden we were enveloped by a cloud of fog. It had come out of nowhere. There hadn't been any fog anywhere before that very moment. (It was the end of July) It was as though it descended upon us. We drove through it quickly--and we were off the mountain.

Just moments before I could see the city, so far away, and now it was gone. Just like that, we were off the mountain and driving along on a flat road, going straight, with level ground on both sides.

My niece looked at me and said, not "See? I told you," but rather, "That was really weird!"

I'm telling you that I was not halfway down that mountain; I know that for a fact. And that I feared for our lives!. God brought me through the fog to the other side and off that mountain within seconds of my plea. It was a clear, heartfelt plea. We were all quiet for some time after that, none of us really sure how to understand what had just happened.

There are so many questions that go through your mind at times like that. You ask yourself, did that really happen?

Yes. That really happened.

Chapter 22

Chandler

Okay, I am not really sure how to explain this. Chandler is my fourth child. But the thing is, he wasn't supposed to be born. Ever.

I wasn't able to have him. And yet, I expected him — him specifically, not just "a child" — before I had ever had any children. I always knew I would have him even though my first three kids were completely different babies.

Having children was hard for me. I have endometriosis, which is a condition in which the tissue that's supposed to be inside the uterus grows outside of it instead. Which meant that, with every child I had except the first one, I had to have surgery first to clean me out before I could even get pregnant.

By the time I was 36 years old I had three children, but I still felt as though the last one hadn't arrived yet. It was a feeling that I had had forever. I always saw us as a family with four children. So, after Blake was born when I was 34, two years later I wanted to try for child number four. My husband was not thrilled with the idea, but went along with it anyway.

So we tried and succeeded--for about eight weeks. Then along came the miscarriage. I was heartbroken. That was to be the first of many heartbreaks over the next three years. I would go on to miscarry six more times. I thought I was going to lose my mind. I went to doctors over and over and asked why it was happening. They said it was my age.

I didn't believe them. They said it was normal to miscarry after the age of 35. Okay, but still--seven times? I have to say that the last baby I lost, before Chandler was born, changed my heart. It really took a toll on my emotions. I was counting on that one making it. When I lost that baby, I cried out to God, "Why?" I could *see* this baby. When my husband asked me why I wanted this baby so badly, I had to explain to him how I had already kissed its feet, I had already sung songs to it in the morning. I had already loved it. I was *already* its mommy, heart and soul.

I turned to my Bible and asked God for an answer. I said, *If you are not going to give me this child, I need to know, so that my heart can heal. But if You are going to give him to me, I need hope. Either way I am going to move ahead.*

I opened up the Bible and there it was: "Unto us a son is born." It wasn't something I had searched for; it was the first thing I saw when I opened up the book. So I knew what He was saying: "Buckle up! Here comes your baby!"

So, of course, I expected that baby any day now, right?! Except not only was there no baby, there were no more pregnancies. I thought I was going to lose my mind. I just kept remembering what God had showed me – "Unto to us a son is born." So I was surprised when I had surgery at 41 to have a large cyst removed, and my doctor told my husband, "You never have to worry about your wife getting pregnant again. Not only can she never carry a baby, she can't even get pregnant."

I had stage three endometriosis, which meant no baby, no how. My husband and I had not had protected sex in years, so it seemed as though what the doctor had said was true. But why would God tell me that?

I said to my husband, "I find it hard to believe that God would lie to me." Still, it all looked like exactly what the doctor had said. I had not been able to keep a viable pregnancy for the last seven years, and for the past few years I couldn't even conceive. I remember looking into my husband's eyes and saying, "I know I am supposed to believe my doctor, and I know that everything that is being said is true, but it doesn't matter! What I can see is, my faith is real. It is His promise to me that is real."

My husband shook his head and told me to get over it; I was too old and damaged to ever have a child again, so I should appreciate the ones I had. But I giggled and said,

"God can heal anything broken. If He said He is giving me a child, then buckle up. Because he will!"

"I feel sorry for you," my husband said. "You don't live in reality."

So does that mean he called me crazy?

Chandler O'Neill was born March 21, 2007, without the aid of any fertility drugs. And get this: as close as we can figure, I got pregnant the day we had that talk!

Do not let anyone ever tell you that the impossible can't happen, when you have Jesus in your life. God granted me that baby because I asked Him. He answered and I believed Him. It didn't come right away; it came in His time, not mine! But it came.

Chapter 23

My Doctor

I would like to start off by saying that doctors are not my favorite people, and medical attention is not my favorite thing in life. I have an unusual chemistry, and have had a hard time getting medics to listen to me. So the only doctor I have regularly employed is a OB-GYN. I've had the same one for almost twenty years. And when I have an appointment, I usually don't even see the doctor herself, but rather her Physician's Assistant (PA).

So it came as a big surprise when God woke me up one night and asked me to pray for her.

I was baffled. It was 3:00 in the morning, and suddenly God shows me that my doctor is sad, crying, going through a difficult time. So I said, "Okay, I'll pray for her." Which I did.

Then, a few days later, I'm making my bed and suddenly God asks me to stop and pray for her *again*. I wondered, "Really?" Bear in mind that I was not particularly close to this woman. I saw her maybe once a year. And I'm not sure she is even a Christian! But you know me: When God tells me to do something, I (almost always) do it. So again, I listened and followed with prayer--although this time I thought, *Something's up.*

God ask me to pray for her one other time, and I saw her crying about her life, and how she was afraid that God was disappointed in the decisions she had made. I was heartbroken for her, and thought about calling her. But I also thought she would think I was nuts. So I wrestled with the decision for months. Finally I decided not to say anything. It would have been too intrusive and weird--and besides, I probably wouldn't see her again, because I was done having children. If I went into that office I would most likely see her PA. So I finally came to peace with just not saying anything to her, and just confined my involvement with her to prayer.

Then I had an ultrasound done. The specialist told me to get to my OB-GYN and have a polyp taken out. I dragged my feet over it for about eight months, until finally one day he called me on a follow up and yelled at me to go. So I went. And guess who I saw. That's right: NOT the P.A., but the OB-GYN herself.

I started sweating, thinking of all the prayers I had prayed for her and wanting to ask if she was alright — and thus running the risk of her thinking I was crazy.

So I thought, "Okay. Let's bring the crazy."

She came into the room and proceeded to tell me how I had waited a very long time, and should have come in sooner. (By the way, she was right.) I listened, and said that yeah, maybe I should have...And then I asked how she was. She said fine. So I asked if perhaps she was going through something difficult.

She stood up and very sternly asked me, "Why?"

I very uncomfortably told her that God had woken me up and asked me to pray for her. That He had showed me an image of her crying.

She said, "Yes. I'm going through a messy divorce after 36 years of marriage."

So we had a nice chat. I told her that God had showed me that she was concerned that He wasn't happy with the way she had led her life, even though she was wrong, and God had been pleased. I asked her if she was a Christian, and she said yes. She was not only a Bible-believing Christian, but she really lived her faith.

I was amazed that all these years I had gone to her and had never known her walk. I also found it strange that God would use me to pray for her. But He knew she needed to be prayed for by someone who didn't know her that well, who could tell her that she was loved and that He was watching over her.

It was very hard for me to tell her that God had spoken to me, and had asked me to pray for her. But I knew that, even if she decided I was nuts and I had to find another doctor, this was the reason I was in her life, as her patient. Luckily — and thank God--she didn't think I was crazy!! In fact, by the end of our talk, she was in tears, with gratitude.

Flash forward a few years: The doctor left her practice and moved. So for 22 years I had had a great doctor, whom I trusted--and not only her, but her assistant-- and now I trusted no one!

I had gotten her assistant's cell number so that we could keep in touch, and so that when she moved I could go with her. After that whole experience I had made a promise to God that when He put someone on my heart and asked me to pray for them, I would reach out and let them know that I was praying for them. So when I was bending down in my closet, cleaning out my large quantity of shoes, and I saw my doctor's assistant crying, my reaction was, "Ugh! Really? Why?"

I thought, *She is the sweetest thing ever!* But I just moved along to my huge Imelda Marcos task of going through my shoes--when suddenly I heard God say, "Brittany", I thought we had a deal. When I put someone on your heart, you were going to pray for them."

I said, "I know, God. I am so sorry! I'll do it right now." So I did. I said a snapshot prayer and moved on.

Well.

A few hours later I was cleaning my bathroom, and as I reached down I suddenly saw and felt the dread that had come over this woman. It actually brought me to tears. I said, "Lord, I am so sorry. She is really hurting and I didn't take it seriously. I am so sorry." From that moment on I started praying and praying for her. I asked God to heal her saddened heart. I prayed and prayed.

But when I picked up my phone to call her, once again I felt doubt! I thought, *What if I'm wrong, she's going to think I'm crazy! Actually, she's going to think that even if I'm right.*

I heard God say, "Do what I expect of you, not what you feel."

It is really hard to stick to your mission in life when you are more worried about yourself and what other people think of you, than doing what God asks of you. Because then that whole free will thing comes into play. So I thought, *I'll just text her, and ask if she's ok.* So I did. No answer. I got in the shower and my phone rang. And I heard God say, "That's her, and she is leaving you a message and telling you she's doing great. And she is not. Call her back and let her know she is Pinocchio-ing you."

I got out of the shower, dried off, and sat there and listened to the message. In her charming, bubbly voice she told me how great she was doing, and thanked me for my concern. She didn't sound distraught at all. I figured I was wrong. I was hearing voices in my head, and started wondering if I needed a high-priced shrink!

At times like that, you have to reach deep down into your soul. You're either a believer or you're not. So who am I? Do I call her back and tell her that I saw her crying, and risk her thinking I'm a nut? Do I tell her that God has asked me to pray for her, and that she is loved and watched over?

Then God said, "Do you not trust Me?"

By then I was crying. Because, honestly, this was really hard for me, and I didn't want to do it. But I dried my tears and picked up the phone and called her back. She was as bubbly as ever, telling me she really loved her new job but she missed her friend, the doctor. So I took a deep breath and tell her, "I see you. I see you crying. God showed me your broken heart—"

--and all of a sudden she burst out in tears. She confessed that she cried every day. She missed her best friend, and for the first time in her life, she felt lost. Her cry was deep and heartfelt; it matched the sadness that God had shown me. We talked. I told her she was going to be fine, and that all would be well. I reminded her that God loved her and watched over her. She was never alone.

I know she was grateful. I told her that I wasn't psychic. I didn't know the future. My only message was that God loved her and was with her.

This contract or agreement I have with God is the hardest thing I have ever done in my life. It is very hard to tell people what you have been told and not have them think you are a witch! Nonetheless: Do what you've been asked. Do what you know you are to do, no matter what the consequences. God needs his soldiers and his warriors. When you are called, answer.

Chapter 24

Cheryl and the Twins

So I get a phone call one day from my girlfriend Cheryl. She's pregnant! Baby number three! How exciting!

Tony and Cheryl had gotten married about a year before my husband and I. I was present at each of her children's births. I really appreciated what kind of couple and what kind of parents they were. They were hard-working. Their kids were involved with everything they did, and they were involved with everything the kids did.

When I saw Cheryl just a few days later, I was amazed to see that she already had a bump. Because normally Cheryl is rail-thin, weighs a buck-five, and has no particular bumps. So it was too soon for her to be showing anything. I said, "Girl, you have twins in that belly of yours!" She giggled and said, "I have a doctor's appointment and ultrasound later today. So we'll see. But shhhhh!"

Later that day Tony called, screaming, "We have twins! We have twins!" He was so excited! I invited them over for a celebratory dinner--the Italian way, with spaghetti. The whole family was so thrilled. And it was funny: Tony had always said that she would have twins. It was almost as though his spirit had prepared him.

Cheryl, meanwhile, was delighted, but also concerned. She said, "I'm happy, but I'm also scared. I'm little! How am I going to carry twins?"

I just laughed and said, "Well, they're in there. You're just going to have to!"

Previously, Cheryl had had fairly uneventful pregnancies. She was a really balanced person, so even though she was still working, I knew she'd balance her way through this pregnancy, too. So I wasn't worried about her at all. I just wanted to make sure I was second in line to see those babies born!

I was in Virginia, at an antique show in the beginning of August. The twins were supposed to be born in September. So I didn't worry--until I was woken up at four in the morning, one night, by God. He asked me to pray for Cheryl. So I prayed for her babies. Then I heard God say, "No, I said, pray for *Cheryl*." I said okay, I would. I got a bit worried. Then I thought, *Well, I'll pray for her throughout the day.*

The next night I started to pray for Cheryl, and I heard the Lord ask me to pray *for her organs*. WHAT? Organs?! What was going on? I got scared. I thought that maybe I should call her or Tony. Then I decided that if I did, it might scare *them*, because I knew I wouldn't be able to disguise how worried and frightened I was. So I didn't do anything. Besides, the next morning I was scheduled to go back home, so I just decided to see them when I got back.

When my husband picked me up at the airport I asked him to get out his phone. He asked me why, and I told him that I was worried about Cheryl, and that God had told me to pray for her organs.

He turned white. He told me that Tony had called him and said Cheryl was in the hospital with preeclampsia.

I said, "Take me there now."

I can't tell you how freaked out I was. I was overwhelmed. I knew that if God was asking me to pray for her organs, then she was in some serious trouble. I went to the hospital and I prayed with Cheryl and Tony over her and her babies.

So. Everything ended up fine. She gave birth to two baby girls six weeks early, and she went home a healthy mother. But I really believe Cheryl had been in some serious trouble, and a blanket prayer was not what she needed. I was glad I had gone through and prayed for each organ, one by one. And even though, while I was doing it, I wasn't sure why, in the end I was grateful that I had. But I have to tell you that, from that day on, I have learned to pray very specifically, and to listen to God without assumptions or preconceptions.

Chapter 25

Be Careful What You Pray For

This chapter is bizarre to say the least.

It all started one day when I was at my kitchen window and I saw a squirrel running across my backyard wall. I thought, *I didn't know squirrels lived in Arizona!* Then, *They can't get into my yard, can they?* I had a six-foot, block wall fence; I was sure they couldn't climb *that*. Right?

Well, needless to say, that squirrel schooled me: The next day I saw that thing shimmy up and down my wall like an escaped convict! For the next few months I enjoyed watching him eat from my fruit trees. He loved my peaches in the summer and the oranges in the winter. I didn't really mind—in fact, I'd have to say I enjoyed it!

Then came springtime, and suddenly one squirrel had turned into three. But they were still cute. So I watched them run amok in my backyard. They'd show up in the early morning, drink out of our ponds and eat until it was nap time, and then leave. This again went on until winter—

--and then spring came, and there were no longer three. Now there were fourteen! And they moved *permanently* into my small backyard. They ate every apple, peach, plum, grape and banana in sight! They took over. It was like the mafia seizing control of a business. And I was terrified to go into my own backyard. All I kept thinking was, *Next year there'll be 40. Or 50.* And *they're going to get into the house.* I felt like I was going to freak out!

So I sat down one morning and asked God, *Please, Lord, please--take them away. I'm scared. And they're creeping me out!*

One week later my dog was outside and I noticed him playing with something. It looked like a squirrel tail. I went out and sure enough--it was. But it was already stiff, so I knew that my dog hadn't killed its owner. The squirrel had been dead before my dog ever found it. Then, as I was looking around, I happened to glance under a pink bougainvillea, and I saw it: the squirrel den.

It looked a bit messed up, like someone or something had been digging in the area. But I really didn't think twice about it until about three days later. That's when I realized that I hadn't seen a single squirrel all day. I went outside and walked around and searched: There were zero squirrels. A few more days went by and I decided to ask my neighbor if he had seen any squirrels, and he said no. They hadn't eaten the food he left out for them. A few days after that I asked my neighbor down the street if *she* had seen any squirrels, and she delivered the bombshell news.

A *bobcat* had come through the neighborhood and eaten them all up!

Gulp.

I can't tell you how that made me feel. I hadn't realized that my prayer had prompted God to kill them all. When I prayed about that, God reminded me about the cycle of life. He also reminded me about being careful what you pray for. It took me a while to get over that, and ever since then I'm certainly more careful with my words!

Chapter 26

My Vacation

It's raining as I write this, and whenever it rains it takes me back a few years, to one very scary rainy night...

But the story really starts a few weeks before that. I was so excited to go on my annual antiquing trip with my best friend, Robin! We had been doing this for over ten years. It always started the same: We discussed where we were going. I'd buy my ticket. And then I'd get giggly for months until September arrived (that's the month we would always go). Up until then I'd pray for safety—and, oh yeah--for great antiques!

This time was different. When I started praying, I asked God to have me do what He pleased. But I was not prepared for what was to come.

We decided to go to the Scotts Market in Atlanta. It was our fourth time going there and we loved it. We always stayed at the same hotel, so we knew the staff pretty well, and...Well, let's just say that wherever Robin and I go, people always remember us, because we're funny and we love to have a great time.

We had just gotten through our second day of antiquing, when we decided we were hungry. We wanted to eat outside the hotel that evening just to try something new. So we started driving around Atlanta, and we got lost! We had no idea where we were or where we were going. We asked a few people for help, but most of them didn't speaking English, so that kind of fizzled. Then we saw a woman who looked like she knew EXACTLY where she was, and who was moving along like a lady on a mission. So we pulled over and asked her where we should have dinner.

First she gave us directions to a great steak house — and, when we went there, we really enjoyed it. But she had also said, "I don't believe in chance meetings. So I think I was *supposed* to meet you, and to invite you to this women's conference at Lewis Gugliono's church. Would you both like to go?" Well, we didn't have anything else to do after dinner, so we said yes. We went. (Funnily enough, we never ran into that kind lady again. Afterwards I always wondered if she had been an angel, although I'm not sure how many angels know anything about steak houses.) We listened to beautiful music and wonderful testimonies from women. It was very refreshing. It made me smile from the inside out!

Robin was kind of quiet the whole evening—the church was a bit on the holy-roller side, whereas Robin was more a Presbyterian type. But she enjoyed it. We went to the hotel and got some shut eye, because we had a whole day of shopping ahead of us.

The next day we had an excellent time. It was to be our last, as we were leaving for South Carolina the following morning. As we started to pack up the car, suddenly another car drove up and several women got out. They started looking at our things (our antique treasures were all over the place, waiting to be packed) and making conversation. They invited us to an all-Black Christian women's ministry conference for women ministers.

Now, I should add here that Robin and I are neither black nor ministers. So we weren't sure they would really want us. But then Robin told me that some women had invited her to a conference in the hotel that morning, too. It was obvious that we should go. So we did!

First of all, those women looked like they had just come off a movie set. They were dressed in their best and all were amazingly beautiful. Second, I heard what was by far the best music I have ever heard live. Believe me, there was some Holy Spirit moving in that room! Finally, the night featured the best speaker I had ever heard—so much so that, two weeks later, I bought the cd recorded from that evening.

I certainly felt the presence of the Lord almighty. It was amazing! I thought, *Lord what do you have in store for us?* Well, the ladies invited us back for the next morning. But we got up late and didn't want to interrupt by coming in after they had started, so we went down to breakfast. And we recognized one of the ladies who had been in the congregation the night before. Her name was LaDawn. She also had gotten up late, so she invited us to sit with her and we fellowshipped for the next two hours.

Okay, Lord, I thought. *So far You have gotten us three times. Something big must be coming!* Of course I thought it was going to be some great antiques.

For the next few days we traveled through South Carolina. We visited my friend Jim, who once again took us to some amazing antique shops. I couldn't have been happier. I was loving life! Then we were off to Virginia, to Robin's house. This was always my favorite part of our trips, because Robin and her husband had built this beautiful house from the ground up. I mean they had literally built it themselves. It had been a dream she had had, and she and I used to talk about it, and it was amazing to see it come true.

So. It was about nine o'clock at night, rainy and cold. Robin and I were driving on the winding mountain roads of Virginia. It was coming down pretty hard. There was a car and a semi-truck in front of us. Suddenly they both slammed their brakes and came to a full stop. So did we. We sat for a moment. Then and I saw the lady in front of us get out of her car. I asked her what the problem was, and she said she thought that the semi had hit a deer or something. So we sat back down. And then the semi driver began walking up toward us, very slowly and with what I would call a very white face. I rolled down my window and asked him if he was okay.

He said, "Yes. But I think I hit a man."

"WHAT!" I yelled.

Then, all of a sudden, I saw his face get even whiter. He was having some kind of reaction to all this. I thought he was going to have a heart attack. So I asked him to go back to his truck and wait.

Robin and I ran out of the car--and then fear started to take over. The memories of a few car accidents that I had helped out with started to come up, and it made me want to freeze and, maybe, not even get involved. I heard the lady yell, "I found him! And he's responsive!" I thought, *Well, that must mean whoever the truck hit is in one piece, Thank God!* So we ran up to where the woman was hovering over the victim.

Robin started to ask him his name and what he was doing on this Interstate. I started to pray--and then I looked at his body. His torso from the waist was facing up. From the waist down, his legs were facing toward the road. His stomach was distended and I saw blood on his shorts. I realized that he was bleeding internally. Throughout all this, he spoke as normally as if he'd been grocery shopping. I realized he was in shock, and probably dying.

So I sat down and held him. It was very cold and we were both shaking. He had no shirt on, only the shorts. I asked him if he knew God. He laughed—and then he started crying. He said, "I love Jesus, ma'am, but I'm going to hell. I have been a bad man all my life."

I asked him if he wanted to be saved, and he cried out, "Yes! I want to go to Heaven!"

So we said the sinner's prayer together. Then he looked at me so sincerely and said, "I don't want to die."

I believe with all my heart that the Spirit of Death was there to take him. I could feel it. And so could he. So we prayed and asked God to please allow him to live and to change his life. I felt a wave of sheer sincerity radiating from him, and the true love of our Lord Jesus Christ. Then I looked up, and was stunned to see that the ambulance drivers and the people around us had taken their hats off, and were praying with us and giving the Lord respect. Then they took him away.

I spent the next few days in bed at Robin's. I was completely broken out in hives and freaked out. But we asked after that man and we learned that he had survived. We were able to track him down, and when we spoke to him he told us that it was going to take about a year, and a series of surgeries and therapy, but that he should be able to walk again.

Looking back, I feel as though God had prepared us for what was going to happen. Somehow, our encounters with those ladies—the one we asked directions of on the street, the gathering at the church, and the breakfast with LaDawn—had given sound minds and hearts just when we would need it most, in that terrible emergency. I know for a fact that if I had been my normal self that night, I wouldn't have been able to deal with that poor man.

Because I don't like those kinds of things. They scare me and I usually freeze up. I feel that it was only through the grace of God that we were able to do the right thing that night.

Chapter 27

Blake

I cannot even tell you how hard this chapter is to write.

Being pregnant with my son, Blake, was one of the most difficult times of my life. It was a year filled with fear and faith--and the amount of each that I experienced fluctuated every day. I was at a job that I really needed to quit. I felt abused and misused. I had two children at the time — two girls, ages four and twelve. I really had wanted another baby, but I felt that if I got pregnant at that job, it wouldn't be good. So there was a lot of stress.

And I was exposed to a lot of chemicals in the air, from the new carpets in the manufactured homes I was selling. Still, I was addicted to the money I was making. So it was almost worth the abuse and the poor quality of life I was experiencing...

Until finally, one day, I had had enough. I backed my car up to the office, popped the trunk, and hauled my belongings through the glass doorway and threw them into the car. I was free at last! And what happened that night? I celebrated with my husband—who didn't celebrate back. In fact he was completely freaked out that I had quit my job without having another one lined up.

But I have to tell you (like I told him), that's the way it had to go down. I had prayed and prayed about quitting my job all that year, and I was told very clearly to quit without having another one. My husband told me I was hearing voices, and that God would never to tell me to do something so financially careless. But I had saved $13,000 in what I called "hush money" that I never told him about, just so that, if I ever had to quit, I could do it without hurting us.

I stayed home for the next three months. At the beginning of the third month I was talking to a friend that I used to work with, and she mentioned that she didn't feel so good. When I asked why, she told me she had her period. I said "WHAT!?" I had been enjoying my time off so much, I had forgotten that I was supposed to have one of those! And I couldn't remember the last time I *had* had one!

I called my husband and told him to bring home a pregnancy test after work. Well, he was so excited, he left work early and got one right away. I took the test and, lo and behold, I was pregnant!

We were thrilled. My husband's first reaction was, "There's my boy!" I wanted a lot of kids, and had certainly been wondering when that next baby was going to come, so I was more than excited, too. (I didn't know how hard this was going to be, or I might have been afraid instead of excited.)

The thing was, though, I was almost three months pregnant and was supposed to start a new job in banking *the next day*. But once I realized I was pregnant, I also realized that something was different. I was gaining a lot of weight really fast, whereas with the other two babies I hadn't. There were other things as well, and I knew something was wrong. We had found out that morning that I was 19 weeks pregnant—and that the baby was the boy my husband so desperately wanted! He was beside himself. He told me. "I'm leaving and going to buy a football!" (Funnily enough, to this day neither he nor my son have ever thrown one.)

After the doctor's appointment I was at work, and I noticed that my breathing had changed, and that I had started cramping. I was afraid to tell my husband, though, because he had already lost a child. I went to the hospital, where they said I was in labor and, because I wasn't 20 weeks pregnant yet, they could do nothing for me--or even attempt to stop the labor.

I was freaked out. I went home and didn't say a word. I just started praying obsessively. "God, please save my child. Make him yours. Give him a purpose in this life that will give You honor. Make him a man of God." I made it through that night, and about three more weeks--until I ended up at the hospital. I was there all day before I broke down and called my husband at eight o'clock that night. He rushed down to the hospital to find out that they were going to medevac me to a different hospital. He turned colors and said he wanted to leave. He told me he was going home. He was tired and would see me tomorrow.

Needless to say, that went over like a fart in church! I told him I couldn't do it alone. He looked at me and said, "I can't be afraid in front of you."

My heart broke for him. I knew he was in more emotional pain than I was in physical pain. He went to the other hospital with me, but then, with my blessing, he went home.

(Ladies: Men are human. They have to grieve, and sometimes that grieving has to be private.)

I understood that--and thank God I did, because what came next would not have flown with him. I knew in my heart something was really wrong. I didn't know what it was, but I knew that my maternal instincts were aroused, and I wasn't letting anyone near my baby! So when I got to the hospital and they went to check me, I said no!

They said, "You are in active labor and we need to check you."

I said, "Give me the release. I'll sign it. But you're not checking me!" When they asked why, I said, "Because you'll cause my baby to be born. And I don't want that yet."

The nurse looked at me and rolled her eyes. They put me on magnesium; it burned like a hot poker going through my veins. I cried like a wounded animal! Then they sent in the doctor, who told me that they were going to be giving me a steroid shot. I knew right then and there: No way. It wasn't that I was opposed to the shot; I had had one with the previous pregnancy. I just *knew* I couldn't have one with this baby.

They tried to tell me that the decisions I was making were going to kill my baby. I said, "No. If I let you give me that shot, *that* will kill the baby."

The next morning the doctor ordered I be taken down to the neonatal unit, so that I could see what a twenty-four-week-old baby looked like. So I saw. Her name was Kathryn, and did it scare me, absolutely. But I didn't budge.

The doctor came in a bit later to talk with me. She told me the same thing: "You are risking the life of your child."

I remember looking out the window and praying in my heart for God to help me be strong, to do what I knew was right. I looked at this doctor and asked her very clearly, "Do you love my child?" She gave me a very strange look, and I repeated, "Do you love my baby?"

She said, "No."

I said, "Well, I do. I have already kissed this baby. I have already loved this child. And as God as my witness, I know that if you give me that steroid you will kill my baby." I said, "I don't know how I know, but I know."

She looked at me and asked if she could ask me some questions off the record. I agreed. She was a Hindu, from India. She said, "I believe you. I just have requirements that I have to follow." She asked if I had particularly bad allergies.

I told her that I did--especially with this pregnancy! I sneezed sometimes 50 times a day. She said she had seen mothers with particularly high allergies go into labor early. She encouraged me to work on the allergies and maybe things would work out.

They released me a week later--and I delivered the baby. He was just a week early! I took my new son home and kissed his feet and loved on him just like I knew I would. But when he was about a week old, I kept thinking, *Something is wrong. I can feel it in my heart.* I prayed over him and prayed over him. I asked God to protect him from everything. I reminded God of my prayer, to make him a man of God so he could bring honor to His name.

It turned out that, from the time he was a week old, Blake suffered from a rare disease called spontaneous anaphylaxis. With this disease, suddenly--for no reason at all--you can stop breathing. It is almost unheard of in children and is usually deadly in adult onset. Blake has a particularly high allergy to most medications, and if I had taken that steroid it surely would have ended his life.

I am grateful for God's grace in my life. I am grateful for the strength He lends me. I am even thankful for the fear He allows me to be in, even though there is no need to fear when faith is involved. On average Blake misses 60-80 days of school a year. He struggles almost every day. He is genuinely a man of God and is a truly compassionate soul. I look forward to watching him grow into his role in God's world!

And always know, son, your Mommy loves you!!

Chapter 28

Thank God for Steven

This is a truly crazy story.

It's one of those almost-took-the-wrong-turn-in-life stories, about a decision that would have caused my life to go in a completely different direction. I'm positive if it weren't for God sending his angels to protect me, I would be divorced again--and devastated.

After my divorce at the ripe old age of 22, I began what would turn into years of counseling and recovery meetings, trying to get over my divorce—and, quite frankly, my childhood. I realized that I didn't want to make any more decisions based on what I had learned as a child or, for that matter, decisions based on anger. I had read what literally seemed like a thousand books on how to retrain the behavior I had been taught. I had to unlearn and re-teach myself everything, from how I tried to control people around me, to the recurring urge to vacuum my cat. (I'd had a need for perfection.)

It was a fresh start to a life that had had a very hard beginning. I would have given myself an A+ on my progress, but I'd earned it. I studied hard and was determined not to make the same mistakes my family made.

So I proceeded to date John, a nice guy who was very unavailable.

He worked all the time (or he said). He only had time to see me every so often. But the thing is, I really liked him a lot. In fact I wanted to marry him! We dated for about two years--not all the time, of course, because he (claimed he) didn't have time, but enough so that I really thought we were heading in the right direction.

However. Through various other women I found out that he wasn't such a great guy. It turned out he had been dating me *secretly*, and telling everyone that we weren't dating and were just friends. ("Friends"? For two years?!)

So I moved along and met Steven. He was the complete opposite. He wanted to see me all the time, and did. Steven and I dated for about three years, during which time he never talked about marriage — which, after a while, got to be too much. I'm the girl you marry, not the girl you date for life. I wanted more children and a complete family, and I wasn't going to let my heart, and any emotional weakness, get in the way of making what I knew was the right decision. I decided that if Steven didn't want to marry me, someone else would.

Which left me wide open for the next one waiting around the corner—the devil himself.

I went out with my coworkers one night and here came John. *Again.*

I knew when he saw me that he missed me. (How could he not! I'm a great girl!) He asked me if he could talk to me. I said no. Then he said he just wanted to apologize for the way he had treated me. Well. I have to admit, that made me go, *Hmmmm.* I'm as interested in a confession of unworthiness as the next girl! And then John went from "I did you wrong" to "I'm sorry and I'm ready for you, and ready to get married now"!

Married? Well, that was the word I was looking for. I didn't know what to say other than, "I'm with Steven. And you had your chance." He asked me if Steven had asked me to marry him yet, and I said no. John said that Steven was a fool just like he had been, and if just gave him another chance he would make it right with me.

I left, overwhelmed. I went to Steven and asked him if he had ever thought of getting married to me—or getting married at all. He said he wasn't interested in getting married. I was devastated and shocked. I had thought for sure we were going to get married.

There are times in your life when you more or less fall to your knees and pray that you don't make the wrong decision. This was one of them for me. To sum it up: I had been with a man for three years who didn't intend to marry me, and I was now being sought after by a guy who I once *wanted* to marry, who now claimed that he had seen the light and wanted to make all my dreams come true! That's what you call a conundrum!!

And now, of course, having never run into John for three years, I was running into him all the time. At one point he asked if we could just please talk, and I said no, that I was going home. So he walked me to my car--and we ran into someone he knew, and introduced me as the girl he should have never let get away. He said, "She wanted to marry me and I was a fool and I have regretted it for the last three years." He turned to me and said, "I missed you, Brittany. Please, please give me another chance."

I left very confused. I thought, *Is this God intervening in my life? What is going on with me?*

I was so stressed out, I woke up at 5 in the morning and started cleaning my house. All I could think of was, *I am with someone that doesn't want what I want and I have someone else who does want what I want.* So at 5:30 in the morning I called my life mentors, Bill and Agnus. I was in tears and they told me to come over. (Thank God for great friends.) I drove over to their home and, on the way, I asked God to please let me not make a mistake with my life, to not let me take a wrong turn. I told Him that I needed a clear answer.

When I got to Bill and Agnus's house I sat there and explained to them, in tears, what was going on. I would like to say most of those tears were because I had just come to the realization that Steven wasn't thinking of me as a wife, and I was freaked out. I was also facing the agony of yet another breakup. So I explained to them my dilemma. They knew both men; they had met Steven with me a bunch of times, and had done business with John. So I thought that they would have good input on the situation.

So there I am: Sitting at their kitchen table, crying and praying and listening to two of my most favorite people. This went on for about an hour. Then, at about 6:30 in the morning, there's a knock at their sliding glass door. It's their friend, Dee Dee. Now, I don't know about you, but I don't typically have unexpected guests, and definitely not *two* of them before seven in the morning! I am, of course, embarrassed—my eyes look like I've become a vampire, and my nose is the size of Canada and, I'm pretty sure, dripping with a cascade of snot. Oh, and did I mention that I drove over in my pajamas? In short, I'm a hot mess.

So Dee Dee walks in and—quite reasonably--is stunned. She doesn't really know what to say. It is obvious that I am upset. In fact, now I'm hyperventilating. So this sweet woman, who has never met me in her life, sits down and asks me what's wrong. And I start spilling my guts, telling her about the bird in hand and the one in the bush.

And she gets this strange look on her face.

She says, "This is really crazy. My boss, Shirley, is going through this same thing--except *she's married,* and being pursued by this guy who wants to marry her." I said I felt so sorry for her. Then I go on to explain that this guy was a contractor, and that he did work for our company and that's how I met him...

And Dee Dee has this look on her face like she had been suddenly hit by a bat. She says, "That's weird! My boss's guy is also a contractor. And she met him at work, too! He asked her to leave her husband and said that he would marry her."

Then I told her about how John had told someone that I was the one who got away. And she looked at me and said, "What is this guy's name?"

And guess what. Prince Charming was using this same line on a different girl! WHAT A CREEP! I asked her what her boss's name was, and she told me, and get this--it was a girl that I knew very well! Talk about a close call! I was in shock—and then I started laughing. I thought, *Thank God I pray about everything I do. I could have really screwed my life up!*

I reflected on what and why this had happened, and I concluded that in fact this whole escapade was a good thing. It really brought to light what I wanted for my life. It made me really aware of how much I wanted to be married and have children. Of course, it took Steven a year and a half more to marry me—but in the end, *he* was my Prince Charming. And while I'm sure you're wondering, did my husband have a clue about all this and about what almost happened, the answer is yes. I told him everything!

The moral of the story? Pray, pray, and pray--*especially* about any life changes.

And, of course, thank you, God, for Steven!

Chapter 29

Crazy Crazy Crazy

Okay, this is one for the this-is-just-crazy books. I'm in shock that it actually happened. But this story ought to show you that God really does listen to your prayers.

This was a different kind of prayer. I grew up in a really small town (of 1,200 people) in a not very populated state. It was like being raised in a subculture. My husband, when he met me, asked me if I was neighbors with the Cleavers of *Leave it to Beaver*, or if Andy Griffith was sheriff of my hometown. He had a hard time with the concept of people actually saying what they mean and being held accountable for their behavior.

I do believe he told me on more than one occasion that I was the weirdest girl he had ever met. (My answer was, "Maybe. But look who keeps coming back!") His first you-are-weird experience came when he spent two hours on my porch, drinking lemonade, because I had no alcohol--and then, when he wanted to come into my house and use the bathroom, I said no and told him to go home. I should probably tell you that he was a wild boy: he had long hair, an earring, a tattoo, and was in a band! Compared to other boys in our town he was Keith Richards. So there was no way I was letting that wild boy into my house!

That should tell you (as it told him) just how sheltered I was and how really very carefully I behaved. Mind you, when I moved to a city, I adjusted to urban life just fine. But there was always this sadness that things weren't like when and where I grew up.

In our town, on Christmas, all the neighbors brought us cookies. Families went to the river on Saturday morning and spent the weekend. If you moved into the neighborhood, people brought you a gift or a casserole. Everyone washed their cars in their front yard on the weekend. And people in that little town cooked some of the best food you have ever tasted in your life. In fact, I think it ruined me for any food I was to have anywhere else. I don't think I've had one satisfying meal since I left!

So different was my childhood compared to my city life, that I would sometimes go through bouts of sadness-- especially for my children. I wanted them to experience a fun street dance, or a great homemade doughnut, or what it was like to know everybody in town.

And so, one particular week, I was feeling glum and blue in just this way, and found myself, not really *praying,* but talking to God. I told Him what parts of my childhood I missed. I said that, above all else, I longed for the atmosphere of my hometown. I told Him that if He could just bring me a piece of it, I would really appreciate it.

What did I expect? Oh, I thought maybe God would have me find a cafe that reminded me of home, or cause me to see some kids playing in mud, or spot a family taking a trip to a lake.

But never did I expect what He did for me!

I came home from a late day out with my family. It was around nine at night. My husband took the kids into the house and I went to the mailbox to get the mail. Now, the house next door had been for sale for a few months, and lately I had noticed that a Sold sign had gone up. But I decided that the new owners must have started moving in while we were out.

I walked by and noticed that people were in the newly-sold place. On the way back I saw a really tall man in the doorway. But, because the porch light was on and the bright light was shining in my face, all I could really see was his silhouette. The figure was tall and stately-looking. In fact, he looked familiar—like my old friend Scott (not his real name), a pal from my hometown. He graduated with my brother and I graduated with his. Scott used to come over to my house after school, and he and my brother used to tease me and get me to chase them. But, I thought, it couldn't be Scott.

Then I heard him yell my name.

I couldn't believe it. It *was* Scott, and he had moved in next door! Now, more than a million people live in my city, so what are the chances that he would move in *right next door?*

I had asked God to bring me some of my hometown and man, did He — he brought in Scott and moved him in next door! Unbelievable!

I would like to note that most of my prayers consist of me just talking to God, like he's my best friend, and we're having just a laugh, sometimes. (Or a cry.) I treat Him as though He is real and in front of me. My faith in Him is real and I believe He is alive, and well, and always present.

Chapter 30

God Lost One of His Sheep

As a mother, I find that this chapter breaks my heart.

I first asked my oldest daughter if I could write it, because it is very personal to her—actually, to both of us. It's about a tearful time, but one that we got through. She felt that it was important for me to write because I told her I think it will help a lot of mothers and their teenage daughters.

When she was graduated from high school she had never really been in love. She had dated a guy who was an Orthodox Jew, and I'm not sure who was more upset-- his mother or her father. I liked the guy she was dating, and besides, I had been praying for her since the day she was born, and I wasn't going to worry about it. I honestly thought that my God is great and all things work out for the good.

She had gone to a party one night and came home screaming, "I found the man I'm going to marry!" Then she said, "Actually, mom, the first thing he said to me was, do you want to marry me!" She was so excited. She said, "Mom, you're never going to believe how beautiful he is."

I said, "Beautiful is a strange word for a guy."

She said, "He *is* beautiful, mother!"

She had never been even five minutes late for a curfew. She had really never disobeyed me or refused anything I had ever asked of her. She was a great kid — 'til she met that boy…

I would just like to state that this is the only time in my life I actually thought of hiring someone to beat someone up. I know what you're thinking: "You're a Christian!" Why yes, I am. But I'm an honest one! I had my perfect daughter--who was a virgin--staying out all night, and I was freaking out!

It was about three weeks into the love of her life (or so she thought), and I was losing my mind. I wanted my beautiful 19-year-old smart, well-behaved daughter back. I invited the boy over with the intention of making sure he knew exactly how crazy I was and exactly how far I would go in making sure he did not taint my perfect child.

Well, I have to say, after my extremely strong talk with him, she was never late again. And, by the way, he definitely *was* beautiful. They were going along terrifically, like they had known each other their whole lives. I thought, *Wow, this might actually be the one!* He hadn't gone to college, nor did he have a car, and he didn't seem to be very motivated in life — or at least not about the same things she was — but he was just the nicest guy, with the sweatiest soul. It was exactly what she needed.

Now, my daughter is extremely motivated; she wanted to be an astronaut and see every corner of the world. Her father and I talked to her about this relationship, but her mind was made up. So we told this boy, "If you're going to be in her life, you have to go to college." He agreed. We were happy.

I never worried about her having sex before marriage, because she had made an oath not to do that. I had talked to her about it because she had been keeping late nights, and she told me, "Mom! Seriously. Don't worry about it. I would never do that!" So I went along and honestly didn't worry. She was coming home on time, and we really grew to love him.

I was praying one evening, and I had her on my heart, and so I asked God to please reveal to me who my daughter was. It's not that I was worried. She was asleep in her room. I just thought I'd ask.

Well, there should be a chapter in the Bible that warns mothers to either take a Xanax before praying that prayer, or just an all-out exclusion on the ability to ask that question. Because I'm telling you, you will never believe when He answers you. You're going to believe He has got your daughter mixed up with someone else's! Because I went to bed after praying that prayer, and at about three o'clock in the morning, God woke me up. (I do really wish He could find a better time, but that seems to be the time He gets my attention the most!) So I asked, "Lord, what is it, 'cause I am so tired…"

He told me to take my bible downstairs and open it. I thought, *What in the world is this? He usually just tells me what's wrong. Why is he having me read?* Well, I got a glass of water, and I sat down, and I opened up the Bible, and there it was: I HAVE LOST ONE OF MY SHEEP.

I almost threw up. I knew instantly what He was saying--that my daughter had broken her vows. I was devastated. And then I was a little crazy. And then I went back to being devastated. This went back and forth a few times. I cried and cried and I prayed and prayed. I was so sad. All I could think was, *Hadn't I taught her the right way?* I had! So what happened?

The truth was, she was human, and she acted like a human. And, since God forgave her, *I* needed to forgive her, and not make her feel like she was a leper or a harlot and that she was going to burn in hell. This is where the compassion of Christ comes in, and as a Mother I had to ask God to fill me with it. I had to make sure that she hadn't turned her back on God because she was sinning. As a mother, my head was spinning, but as a Christian, my heart was trying to adjust to speaking the truth to her without shaming her. The end result had to be that she made her own decision.

God does not command us to love Him; He gives us free will. She needed to come to terms with Him on her own and make her own decisions. So, after two hours of crying and praying, I went upstairs and woke her up and asked her to come downstairs and talk to me. She said, "Mom, really? It's five in the morning." But I insisted, so we went downstairs.

I started out by saying to her, "Honey, God woke me up and told me He had lost one of His sheep." I said, "You are having sex."

She said, "No, Mother, I'm not."

I said, "Honey, God *told* me." And I read her the passage. I said, "God told me you are having sex."

She said, "No, I'm not!"

I said, "Honey, you and I both know what He is saying to me."

Then she said, "God is lying," and as soon as the words left her mouth, she realized what she had said, and she burst into tears. She asked for forgiveness. I explained to her that her decisions, at her age, were between her and God, but I didn't want her lying to me anymore.

I told her, "You need to be responsible and get on the pill. Or, quit having sex. It's up to you." I gave her the phone number to my OB-GYN and told her to make an appointment, to be a responsible adult and make responsible decisions.

I would love to say that that was the end of it. But her father woke up and heard our conversation and...well, since this is a Christian book, we won't get into what he had to say about the boyfriend! But we never brought it up or spoke to her about it again.

About a year later she came to me and asked if she could talk to me. She told me that she had always felt like what she was doing was wrong, and she didn't want to do it anymore. She was taking herself off the pill and she wanted to rededicate her life. She and the boy dated for about three more years after that.

I never asked her if she went back on her word, because I do believe in the redemption of Christ and believe that at some point children are going to need to go to the Father in Heaven all on their own. We teach our children to lie to us by not accepting their mistakes as just what they are— mistakes. By consigning them to a world of condemnation it makes them emotional putty for the devil to mold, and do whatever he wants them to do. Love and accept your children, mistakes and all. Do not condemn and preach and judge. Love them through it; guide them, and always make it clear that every action, whether good or bad, has a consequence.

Chapter 31

Answered Prayer

I really loved my job. My boss, Tom, was a Christian. He taught me more about how to be a real Christian, and about the effect I had on other people's lives, than anyone or anything before him. He once told me, "Never underestimate the effect and value you have in another person's life. The things you do and say to that person make a difference." He taught me the power of a single word.

I was so sad when my company sold and was bought out by another firm. While all this was going on, I had had my second child. Well, along with a beautiful baby comes a lot of bills. And, worse, we had closed on a home just a few days after she was born. (I strongly recommend not doing that.) So I went from living comfortably to never having any money and really struggling.

Solution? Get a new job!

I was lying in bed, fretting about money, and I decided to pray. Now, I usually pray lying down (or, as it happens, while driving). Honestly, I can pray wherever I am. It's nothing formal, usually. However, at that moment I was really broke, so I decided to kneel on the floor, on my knees—somehow I thought this would make sure God heard me! I prayed a very passionate prayer.

I asked God for a job that would pay me more than $50,000 a year--which was twice as much as I was making. I also prayed that I would love my job, and that it suited my personality, which I knew was...well, let's just say, *particularly different*.

Before I even had a chance to get off my knees, the phone rang. It was a friend of mine, whom I hadn't spoken to in a while. She called to tell me that they were hiring at her job, and she made over $50,000 a year. I said, "Oh, gee, I don't really want to sell manufactured homes. So thank you, but I'll pass."

So for the next nine months I went on job interview after job interview, but never got the job. It was an experience I had never had before. Up until them I had gotten every job I had ever applied for! I kept praying. And my friend kept calling and asking me to come in and at least look at what she did.

One day I said, "Lord, please! Answer my prayer. We are so broke!"

And the phone rang. It was my friend, who said, "Just come down and see what I do! Please!"

I thought (finally), *Well, I guess it wouldn't hurt to go look.*

I went, I looked, and I was shocked. It wasn't anything like I thought it would be! The homes were beautiful and the office was a fun place to work. I applied for the job--and I got it!

The moral of the story? Guess! Hah!

I worked there for over five years and I made a lot more than what I prayed for.

So I'm here to tell you: If you are unemployed, pray! And pray again! And when God answers, listen!

Your Miracle

I have reserved this last chapter for you! I hope that these stories have inspired you to pray big, and that you stand back and expect your prayers to be answered! I pray that you are able to fill these next few pages with amazing stories of your own miracles!

A Final Note

It has been an emotional five-year journey writing this book. I pray that if there are parts of you that haven't healed, or forgiven, or *been* forgiven, this journey of mine will somehow facilitate your finding a road that only God can guide you down, and that in the end peace and love and, most of all, Joy will overtake your life.

Blessings and Love,

Brittany